To Louise.
　　Happy Chr

Do hope you enjoy the read.
Best Wishes from.
　　　　Beryl Parsons.

One Boy's Heroes is the true story of Freddie Parsons, London schoolboy during the blitz of London in the war years 1933 until 1945. The story starts in 1933 when Adolph Hitler came to power at the same time as Freddie Parsons first saw the light of day—the tyrant and the little boy who would eventually be on the receiving end of a madman's lust for power. How that little boy's experiences during the Battle of Britain in 1940 motivated him in later life to track down and meet his hero the fighter pilot of a Spitfire who fought in the clear blue skies on that hot late summer of 1940.

Written to enable future generations of his family to experience the everyday life and dramatic events as he saw them. This is a happy book, for despite the fears of our parents, we children found a paradise in war.

Stories of pre-war Britain, the magic of visits to the music hall of 1938, and the real feeling of how it was living in blitzed and battered London ... The horrors and despair of evacuation, how Hitler's top fighter fired its machine guns in broad daylight on Peckham High Street ... This story is full of explicit wartime events. Some very exciting, most extremely frightening, others hilariously funny. The story continues into the present day meeting of wartime heroes of fighter command who in 1940 were one boy's heroes.

Age four—that innocent look could be quite deceptive

FREDDIE PARSONS

One Boy's Heroes

1995

Published by
Blue Bird Publications
Red Cow Farm
Hartley Bottom Road
Longfield
Kent DA3 8LB

© Copyright Freddie Parsons 1995

ISBN 0-9525633-0-4

Typeset in Palatino 10/12pt by Scriptmate Editions
Manufacture coordinated in UK by Book-in-Hand Ltd
20 Shepherds Hill, London N6 5AH

All rights reserved. No part of this book may be reproduced or transmitted in any form, electronic or mechanical, including photocopy or any information storage and retrieval system, without permission in writing from the publisher.

This book is dedictated to my dear late friend Marie Scott whose enjoyment of my stories and encouragement to put pen to paper resulted in *One Boy's Heroes*. Marie Scott, who was also a child of the war, was much loved and is sadly missed.

Contents

PEACEFUL LONDON OF THE 1930s	9
THE MAGIC OF MUSIC HALL	16
FACE TO FACE WITH HITLER's NAVY	24
WAR	30
BOMBERS OVER LONDON	39
BATTLE OF BRITAIN	47
EVACUATION	57
DAD'S BLACK MARKET	66
REGMA OF LANGLEY BOTTOM	73
BOYS OF THE BLITZ	97
CAMBERWELL BEAUTY	105
CHRISTMAS WITH MY BARMY AUNTS	115
DODGING DOODLE BUGS	127
THE GREAT SHELTER SHOW	138
VE DAY PARTY	149
FACE TO FACE WITH MY HEROES	163

CHAPTER ONE

PEACEFUL LONDON OF THE 1930s

1933 Hitler came to power, at about the same time as I entered the world.

On 27 March 1933, mother held me in her arms, not realising the dangers that lay ahead for us all. Frederick Charles Parsons married Winifred George two years earlier,. Well, that's what they told me anyway. Dad, a short thin man with a funny ducklike walk, managed to attract and marry mother, a tall sensitive woman who towered over him in intellect as well as height.

I was a noisy little brat, always needing constant attention. Very little entertained me for long. I can't say I remember lying in my cot saying I am bored, but I bet I did. All my life I have needed adventures, to seek them out to fulfil life, to achieve. Little did I know that very soon life for me would be absolutely full of excitement, adventures and sometimes a tremendous amount of danger. To be born in 1933 as the world was about to explode into World War Two was pretty poor timing by my parents.

Mum, Dad and little me all lived in a top floor flat in Brixton, the warm friendly safe Brixton of the nineteen thirties.

Dad at thirty years old was unskilled by trade but extremely skilled by nature. Starting his work life as a schoolboy selling firewood from a homemade wooden barrow in the sooty streets of London, he had struggled hard to start his own business, and now had a successful secondhand car sales in the Brixton Road. He had learnt very early in life that you don't get rich out of a wage packet, and to be rich was his goal. After all there was only one way he could go from his start in life—up.

Mother was twenty two years old when I, the apple of her eye, appeared. She met Dad at sixteen, earning her living as a machinist. When Dad came into her life he must have appeared a bit of a big shot to her—buying her clothes, driving her around in smart cars, causing Mum's bullying father quite some concern over her chastity.

'Men don't buy girls clothes for nothing,' he would shout at her.

Well, apparently he was right. Dad had his wicked way with her. Mum always complained that he had seduced her for years after, but now they were married and happy with their new baby boy, little Freddie. I was called little because, Dad also being a Fred, I was the little one. We only stayed in the flat for a short while before Dad spotted a super little shop to rent in a very good main road position. Having a nice little flat above the shop, it made an ideal opportunity to open a pet shop.

It seemed quite strange for a car salesman to open a pet shop but Dad always had an attraction for birds, feathered or otherwise, so here was an opportunity to open his own pet shop, plus the advantage of somewhere to live. As a boy Dad bred pigeons. He found them to be quite profitable. He would sell them on Sunday morning in East Lane, an open market in Walworth Road, Camberwell.

The birds would always fly home the following week, allowing Dad to sell them again on Sunday.

'The perfect business,' he would laugh, never needing to buy new stock.

Once Dad moved in, up went the signs, "Parsons Pet Stores", "budgerigars, parrots, pet food". We sold it all, including used car tyres from five shillings. Dad from an early age had earned his living as a dealer. He liked his birds, but felt he could make quite a bit more money from tyre sales. So he combined the two unlikely trades as one.

Dad's shop, situated in Coldharbour Lane, Brixton, was on the ground level of a large tenement building called Grosvenor Mansions, with some five floors above. Each floor had its own landing, a large iron mangle stood on each floor, with a bleached scrubbed wooden staircase leading from floor to floor, eventually opening up onto the flat roof of the tall building.

Very soon after moving into our shop, one of my earliest recollections was being gathered up in Dad's arms and rushed up to the roof. The night sky was aglow. Over the rooftops could be seen smoke, flames and glowing embers shooting high in the sky. It was the Crystal Palace burning down—Victorian masterpiece in glass and steel, built for the great exhibition in the mid 1800s. I would have been only about three years old but it is still very vivid in my mind.

The people living in Grosvenor Mansions were very poor, slumlike in appearance, always smelling strongly of Jeyes Fluid, paint peeling off the doors, windows on each landing dark and sooty, but I am sure Mum would have been excited to move into a self-contained flat of her very own.

Well, she would have been except for one small problem.

Rats, thousands of them. The reason for the vile creatures infesting our building was that we backed onto railway arches that supported the viaduct that carried the steam trains high above and through the highly populated area of Brixton. In the arches below were many stables, containing horses' carts, corn etc. A perfect breeding ground for rats, and if they felt like a change of diet, all they needed to do was pop into Dad's shop for something tasty.

These rats were everywhere. They would squeak at night as they scurried from floor to floor, run across our beds as we slept, they even ate Dad's socks as they lay on the bedroom floor at night, Dad's socks unfortunately having a flavour that would only appeal to rats. We would chase them around the flat, armed with anything that would inflict a fatal blow to them.

Dad trapped a big brown hairy one against the wall with the head of a bass broom, unsure as to what he should do with him now that he had him trapped. Dad let up on the pressure, the big rat shot straight up the broom handle at him believing that attack was the only defence. Dad lost his nerve and the fat rat lived to eat a few more socks.

In desperation Dad bought a fox terrier, a fast super little dog that killed them on sight, but unfortunately quite often biting their heads off as they peeped out of their holes, leaving the mangled remains to fall back under the floorboards. The smell of a dead rat is something awful. Many times we would prize up the floor to find their decomposed remains.

"Parsons Car Sales" was still going strong, Dad's successful sales forecourt in Brixton Road full of cars that today make your mouth water—Bull Nose Morris, Sunbeams, SS Jaguars. One that Dad used himself had an amazing mascot of a bird with a long neck and beak, its chrome wings would move up and down as the car travelled on the highway.

One amazingly interesting place that Dad would take me to was the car auctions at the Elephant and Castle, a Victorian building. There, regular horse or car auctions were held in the open cobbled courtyard. Dad, looking smart in his grey trilby hat, would check out any interesting cars before the auction started. Prices were quite astounding. Classic cars would fall under the hammer for £3.50, but of course that was over a week's wages for a man in 1937.

Once the auction was over the cars would be driven to Dad's sales front in Brixton Road for the full treatment to prepare them for sale. Now my Dad was the world's greatest bodger. He knew more ways to improve a car than you could possibly imagine.

To name but a few—if a car was bought with holes in the bodywork, Dad's solution, brown paper, (yes, brown paper!) applied with black paint in layers. When dry it became as hard as the surrounding bodywork. Noisy gearboxes or back axles were filled with sawdust, once mixed with the gear oil all grinding sounds disappeared. Bald tyres would have new treads ground into them using a large rotating stone wheel that could cover Dad with rubber dust every time he used it. Once the car had received this treatment onto the forecourt it would go, a whitewashed painted price onto its windscreen declaring it as the 'Bargain of the Week' at only £6.50.

'No, sir, you cannot drive yourself, test drives not allowed...'

'No, sir, there is no money back or guarantee...'

'Don't worry about the brakes sir, they work much better when you are going uphill...'

'Well, what do you expect for six pounds fifty?'

Before you think of Dad a bit of villain, just remember he did not have any advantages in life, his only asset was a strong drive to succeed, and succeed he really did. His friends and other dealers wasted their money with no thought for the future. Dad would tell me many times that they spent their money as soon as they earned it, I saved mine until I had capital behind me. Later in life, they all finished up as they started, owning nothing, paying rent for the rest of their days, riding bikes to work, rolling their own cigarettes with a little machine to save money. Dad had learned from his firewood selling days as a boy, to buy and to sell was the only way to success for him.

My Dad without any intention on his part taught me by example and his stories of how the Parsons family for generations had been working for themselves. All around my father as a boy would have been crushing poverty, not for him the advantage of education, it was sink or swim by his own abilities. But the Parsons family had escaped this trap and for many generations up to the present day, had passed down from father to son the will and drive to run their own business, the search for success is very strong in our blood, and will probably still be there for years to come.

So here was the latest addition to the Parsons line, Little Freddie, starting to learn how we survive. Apart from Dad, I always had characters to learn from like Uncle Dunlop. A dapper little man, sporting a pencil thin black moustache, always smartly dressed in his Burtons suits. Uncle Dunlop's visits to see Dad were always surrounded by quite a bit of mystery. Dad and he would whisper for some time, objects would appear from large holdalls, money would be exchanged. Uncle Dunlop would say farewell amid roars of laughter.

What a nice man he was, my Uncle Dunlop, always so jolly, very friendly to me always. Years later I questioned Dad about my uncle.

'Why, Dad, did I call him Uncle Dunlop?'

Dad roared with laughter ... it was because he stole so many tyres, yes, Dunlops, I never knew his real name but Uncle Dunlop stolen tyre king would visit Dad many times carrying his black holdall, on one occasion containing Rolls Royce flying lady car mascots. My Uncle Dunlop was probably the biggest thief in London.

Years later all Dad's hire cars had Rolls Royce mascots regardless of their make. A villain but a very lovable one, my Uncle Dunlop.

CHAPTER TWO

THE MAGIC OF MUSIC HALL

So with Dad's business going well we were very happy as a family. Living in Brixton in 1937 had one great advantage—the Brixton Empress, a brand new theatre in the heart of Brixton itself. What a place of wonder it was for me, it was just magic, we would never miss even one week, we would walk the quite long distance to be there by 8pm.

What a wonderful sight. I felt spellbound when we arrived, shining black cars everywhere, ladies with black furs, ladies with white furs, stepping from cars, and I mean stepping, these were cars with running boards that you stepped out on. The smell of chestnuts burning from the chestnut seller's coke-filled red hot brazier, the bright lights from the plush red-carpeted foyer, the polished brass shining everywhere, a magic place for me. At the highest point on the theatre building shone a huge illuminated opaque glass star that could be seen from miles around, a truly magical place for a small boy.

On entering the Empress Theatre the excitement grew. Inside the decor was pure Art Deco. On each side of the stalls the walls had deep alcoves with huge statues in gold, back lit for dramatic effect. The smell of new carpet hit the nostrils, we were always booked into the front row centre stalls, just Mum, Dad and me in the best seats in the house. Mum said Dad liked these seats so he could see the girls legs better. In later life I always like the front row seats too, strange isn't it.

There were always big names top of the bill Nellie Wallace, a funny little lady with a feather in her hat, Wee Georgie Wood, a little man playing a boy his mother played by his wife, Old Mother Riley and her daughter Kitty, a great act Old Mother Riley played by Arthur Lucan his wife as Kitty, but the greatest of them all was Max Miller the top comic of his time, this man always worked to full houses every night year after year, he always asked the audience, 'Do you want the white joke book or the blue book?' Everyone screamed blue book for obvious reasons.

But the act I liked best was 'Wilson, Keppel and Betty', probably the most odd act ever. Wilson and Keppel played Egyptians in loin cloths with Betty as Cleopatra. Their act dancing on sand in line in rather a suggestive way, doesn't sound funny—it was hilarious, the whole house fell apart. It was then home after we all stood for 'God Save the King'.

Walking the long walk to Coldharbour Lane and our small shop took us past the pie and mash shop, open late at night then, the smell was wonderful. You need to be Londoner to know what I mean, hot meat pies crisp on top but moist under the pastry served with mash potatoes and liquor, a green gravy made from parsley, or eels jellied or hot, plus hot fruit pies for dessert. We always stopped for a meal after the show and I remember the vinegar and salt on the marble tables which were always old jam jars with holes in their lids, vinegar kept in lemonade bottles with holes in their corks. Why no matching cruet sets you ask? They would have been stolen for sure as soon as they appeared on the tables. The floor of the pie and mash shops were always covered with loose sawdust. Primitive eating it may have been, but so wonderful.

It was at this time that Hitler had come to power. Being so young I was quite unaware how this would affect my life. Hitler came to power in 1933 and was an Aries. I was born in 1933, also an Aries. Hitler's destiny was to rain destruction and terror on our city very soon, but we were so far unaware of any danger.

I had become very fond of friends of my parents, we called everyone Uncle or Aunt in those days whether relation or not. Uncle Max lived on the top floor of Grosvenor Mansions the tenement flats above Dad's shop.

He and his wife were elderly and on entering their home I always wondered what the strange smell was, a sort of musty smell which got stronger as I got closer to his moth-holed old cardigan. He was not a dirty man but remember there were no bathrooms then. A visit there was nice, always lemonade, bread and sugar, and a wave out of their top floor window to the train driver passing through.

My other uncle, Uncle Bob had the hairdresser's shop near Dad's shop. He was a lovable man with two daughters in their teens a visit there was great fun as he always told great stories.

If I wanted a story he would ask his daughter for his thinking cap. This was a large tea cosy fitting down to his ears. With this on he told wonderful adventure stories. One night after a special story involving flying his plane over the Sudan to attack the 'Fuzzie Wuzzies Tribesmen' (stories from our empire days), 'go home, dress up warm and I'll take you there in my aeroplane,' he said.

To my bitter disappointment I was not allowed to return.

As the night light candle flickered in my room that night, I thought how unreasonable mothers can be.

Life was very peaceful and by today's standards slow around the cobbled and wooden tar blocked streets of Brixton—the clopping of the horses, combined with the odd toot from a car horn only breaking the silence.

Mum felt that she could not stay over the shop much longer, rats and all. So the family started looking for a real home, a house. But before leaving Brixton I started to become devious in my own right. One local shop near ours sold toys. In the window was a tin toy gun in black and silver. I wanted it badly. After some weeks, nose to window, I could bear it no longer. On entering the shop I was greeted by the storekeeper with 'Hello, little Freddie, what would you like?' Oh, boy I knew alright.

'Dad said I could have the gun in the window, he will pop along later and pay you,' said I.

To my amazement he gave me the toy. He knew Dad well, their shops only being fifty yards apart, so I pulled it off. Scooting home with my prize the problem was no one must know I had it. Playing and hiding it afterwards became stressful and after about two weeks the game was up. Dad was asked to pay for the gun I remember being told off by Dad. But he probably admired my cunning, so it never seemed a serious offence, just a little con.

So the devious side of my character started to form. Now I learned a new trick. Go to the newspaper shop buy a comic for one old penny, run home as fast as you can, look at all the pictures as quickly as possible, tear back to the shop explaining that I had bought this comic by mistake and already had it at home, so sorry, could I change it for another. Great, two comics for the price of one. I was learning fast.

We also had our family dog at this time—Zuda, a German Shepherd bitch, my first dog. Little did I know in later years I would train dogs for a living and become one of Britain's top dog trainers.

1938

At last Dad had found a house for us, a corner house with upstairs entrance, main road position good possibility for business, 121 Peckham Road, London SE15. Peckham was very nice and to have a main road house was very up market.

The day we moved in was so exciting. It seemed so new but was in fact an end terrace house over 131 years old then, but with all new decorations, new doors etc., so it was new to me. Dad had bought the house for £650 giving £25 as down payment over twenty five years with weekly payments of £1.25.

At age five the most impressive feature was the half glass wooden dividing door from front room to living room. This was very modern to be able to open up to one large room. The house consisted of two floors and a basement, each floor having two rooms on each, the basement had a scullery and kitchen with living room. Our bath was in the kitchen and was filled by attaching a half inch rubber pipe to a gas hand basin water heater in the sink nearby. As you can imagine the bath was big and the pipe was small, it took hours to fill the bath, so on most times we used a tin bath in front of the open coal fire. There was a small outside toilet and a long narrow garden.

The combined kitchen, scullery and bathroom being below ground was always damp, the distempered walls always peeling. We used this one room for everything, cooking, bathing, washing ourselves and our clothes, and it was later to become our air raid shelter as well. The main road position was the attraction for Dad. He immediately saw possibilities for business in such a busy spot—we looked down from our bedroom windows at the trams and buses thundering by, the old square 1932 taxis honking their horns. This would certainly not be the most peaceful spot in the world, but that did not matter. Soon the business signs would appear, the moment Dad was ready to start his car hire service.

Dad's lifelong dream had always been to own a motor coach or car hire business. This spot in Peckham Road would be ideal, nice corner position in a very busy road. There was only one problem—the house was three foot above the road with no garage for his hire car. Dad was not to be put off by such a trivial problem as this. The day after we moved in found Dad with a shovel and bucket, removing tons of soil until it was possible to drive from the road side into his back garden, most of the car was below ground level. If ever the Parsons needed a family motto it would be 'Tenacity'.

Mother just loved the house. This was quite a step for her—from a Brixton flat to her own house. The everyday drudgery was still there for her though. Unfortunately washing machines not yet invented, mother's washing consisted of a bar of green soap and a scrubbing board. Soap flakes shaken from a box with the name 'Lux', the wonder soap flakes, helped when she boiled her whites on the gas stove.

There was one alternative to this terrible hard work— that was the bag wash. A corner shop in Peckham Road was the bag wash shop. Mother would fill a large white bag with sheets, table cloths and any white items. My job would be to drop the bag at the shop on Monday, a few days later to collect the washing whiter than white, unironed and sometimes still warm, the bag having a wonderful fresh bleach smell. These shops were the first to take the burden of wash day from women.

All the bags of washing were sent to the Dutch Boy Laundry Co in Commercial Way, Peckham, where other poor women, sweat dripping from their faces, washed each bag separately in huge boilers, then repacked into your own bag, with a large cardboard label on the string-tied neck. Collecting mother's bag wash was always enjoyable, it paid well, exactly one penny. So with the bag wash over one shoulder and a large jam doughnut in my hand, cost one penny from the adjoining cake shop, I would return to our nice new house, rush in, wash the jam from my mouth, just in time for the children's hour on the radio. I wonder what Larry the Lamb's adventure will be tonight?

Yes, life was so simple then.

ABOVE Winifred Parsons, 1931. An elegant lady of the 1930s

LEFT TOP Little Freddie and girlfriend outside Dad's shop in Brixton in 1937

BELOW Grosvenor Mansions, 1993. I return but the rats have left

CHAPTER THREE

FACE TO FACE WITH HITLER's NAVY

I feel that this is a good time to tell you more about Dad. He was a short man about 5ft 5in, very thin but strong, had short arms, thick and hairy with beautiful hands, not in a feminine way just perfectly formed finger nails, grey green eyes, thin-faced, showed me a lot of affection. When I was very young, he would sit me on his lap, put my head under his jacket and cuddle me. I liked this, it felt warm and nice. It did smell a bit though. As I have said, Dad did not like to bath. Mother was on at him a lot of the time, but he still avoided bathing. Now the smell was not a dreadful body odour, more of a musty smell. That smell was acceptable and part of the enjoyable feeling of being close to my Dad.

Mum was quite tall with dark brown hair. She was taller than Dad, about 5ft 8in, not very big busted but had beautiful long legs with a very attractive shape to them. She had a very sensitive nature verging on being nervous at times, loved to wear furs and large brimmed hats, dressing above her class. Her sisters Ann and Jessie called her the schoolmarm. She did look very smart and would wear fur coats for shopping as well, she told me she always felt good in them. A truly elegant lady of the 1930s. She wore her hair in typical 1930's style—waves down one side, hair smooth and silky, silk stockings and always smart high-heeled shoes would complete her very smart appearance.

Photos of her on our trips to France show her as a tall, slim, smart young woman, with a soft gentle smile, a very caring mother.

An event in 1938 that is still very strong in my memory happened aboard a cross Channel steamer. Day trips to France were commonplace prior to the war. We would drive down to Ramsgate or Margate, hop aboard the most beautiful paddle steamer, with two huge paddle wheels rotating on her sides. The journey to France was slow and leisurely, large wooden deck loungers to relax in made the journey seem like a tropical cruise.

On arrival at Calais we would take coach trips to see the battle ground from World Ward One. On sale everywhere were beautiful mother-of-pearl handled bayonet brooches. Mother returned home with masses of these World War One trinkets for her friends.

Everywhere we went in our coach, we were mobbed by poor filthy ragged children begging for money. Dad would toss a handful of coins out at them each time we stopped. On the last stop I was given the coins to throw as the dirty little faces looked up at us. I held out my hand from the coach windows, felt a sudden snatch and the coins were gone. A woman had grabbed my little hand and taken the money for herself, it is amazing how at only five years of age I clearly remember Dad reprimand that I should have thrown the coins out of the window.

On the return trip back across the channel, thick fog had settled in, it was now dark and as the paddles moved very slowly, we felt very uncomfortable steaming out into the

English Channel. The Captain pulled on his foghorn in a regular and rhythmic fashion, to warn any other ships we were near. All seemed quiet until somewhere in mid-Channel, our paddle steamer brightly illuminated with festoon bulb-covered rigging, received a blast from a foghorn back to her. Our captain immediately hooted again, only to receive a reply back that sounded uncomfortably close.

This signalling continued for some time until along one side of us a deadly black shape emerged out of the silent swirling fog. A German U-Boat submarine! Her captain exchanged words with our ship, using their on-board searchlights to illuminate and check out that we were a pleasure vessel. Our captain became alarmed when our ship lurched heavily to one side at quite a frightening angle. Everyone on board had rushed to one side of the ship to get a better view of the submarine, causing the ship to list dangerously.

'Will passengers please return to the seating areas,' came the call over the intercom.

We did and the submarine slipped back into the fog. A few months later and they would have sunk us. Was this practice for more serious interceptions to come? War was inches away by now.

So here we are, the Parsons family living in the peaceful atmosphere of pre-war 1930s. A very happy time with regular visits to the cinema—Dad dressed in his smart 1930's clothes with grey trilby hat with a large black hat band, trying hard to look like a combination between Fred Astaire and Al Capone, mother pure Ginger Rogers with large-brimmed hats and thick furs.

The music of this time was very special. Men sang with rather strangulated voices giving the 1930s that familiar sound, Al Jolson being the one exception with his booming voice.

'Pennies from Heaven', a very popular song in the 1930s was Dad's favourite, he just loved to sing this song to me. On rainy days he would wait until I was distracted, toss pennies into the air. I would rush around collecting my good fortune, totally convinced that pennies really fell from heaven on rainy days. If it sounds blissful it was, there were no dangers in Peckham to fear in 1938, safe by day or night, we children played in the surrounding streets in perfect safety, totally without any fear.

Peckham Town Hall presented Dad with a first prize for the best garden contest. He really had made a wonderful show using shells and flowers in his new front garden, most of the shells being collected from our regular visits to Southend-on-Sea.

Mother could now really enjoy her shopping trips to Rye Lane, a very smart shopping area in the 1930s, full of good quality shops. The best by far 'Jones & Higgins' departmental store, a beautiful building very ornate in white Portland stone, large revolving doors surrounded by curved glass shopfronts. After spinning round several times in the revolving door, then dragged in by a now irate mother, you would be met by a somewhat stern but polite floor walker. He would greet mother with a 'Good Morning, Madam', in a most affected voice.

The interior of the store was heavenly, fitted with mahogany panelling with large glass-fronted doors, all brass fittings highly polished. Standing in front of the glass-like polished mahogany counter would be huge busted matronly ladies, examining corsets that would easily fit a horse, being served by a cringing shop girl. Always very polite—the floor walkers' beady eyes made sure of that—this was a high class store, and Madam's satisfaction was the floor walkers' main concern. Each department would have its own man in black tails and pinstripe trousers hovering and watching in case any standards were lowered. Mother would swish in, then out again, in her smart fur coat, feeling very special I am sure. It certainly seemed a long way from the rat-infested flat in Brixton.

My sister Jean seemed to be born out of the blue. Having been sent away for a few days, on my return she was just there. Nobody bothered to tell me she was coming. Perhaps they were worried I would ask where she was coming from. I would have to be told about the stork and the gooseberry bush then.

I liked my sister Jean immediately. She had a happy smiling face, no hair, little dimples in her cheeks and earrings hanging from each ear in perfectly formed pearl drops. Jean had been born with little flesh eardrops both matching in size and location, projecting from the exact same spot on her ears that one would fit an earring. They were quite amazing, if they had only been gold she could have kept them for life. Instead they were removed shortly after her birth, leaving no trace.

Jean's earrings had become the talk of the family. My grandmother was convinced that they had appeared as a result of mother, while pregnant, constantly observing a huge barometer on the outside wall of Peckham Town Hall. This barometer was on a painted hoarding and, covering one whole side of the building above the hoarding display, was the slogan of an appeal to local people to support and buy a Spitfire fund, donations received being indicated by a rise in this huge barometer.

When completely full it would show we had achieved the massive amount of £5,000, that amount would have bought us our own Spitfire, when delivered to its squadron with fighter command it would bear our name 'With much pride from the people of Peckham'.

Passing the Town Hall, all eyes would turn to the barometer as we watched the donation rise. This had affected mother's pregnancy ... watching the barometer day after day had produced baby Jean's little earrings. Oh well, life was very simple then, but I must admit they were exactly the same shape as the bomb shape markers that rose on the barometer high on the wall outside Peckham Town Hall.

1938. Dad, Mother and me off to meet Hitler's submarine in the channel

CHAPTER FOUR

WAR

1939

War is declared, so at last we would stop Hitler's progress. But to the Parsons family the war with Nazi Germany meant no change in our peaceful life in Peckham. Things were to happen that would have terrified us had we known—the bombing, the terrible bombing was all to come.

There were posters everywhere saying 'Dig for Victory' or 'Make Do and Mend'—stimulating the people into a defiant mood. But this was the period of the so-called phoney war, just nothing happened. We expected to be bombed within days of war being declared, why did Hitler not strike, shelters were being dug everywhere, a large very deep communal shelter on the lawns in front of the large Victorian building opposite our house.

The Engineering Union Building in Peckham Road, was very deep and safe except for a direct hit from Hitler's bombs. When the first raids came we tried this shelter out on the first night. It was terrible—probably about 300 people below ground, packed together in a hot airless bunker, sleeping on the hard concrete floor with blankets and pillows, huddled in corners trying for privacy, babies crying, people starting to sing wartime songs (like 'Bless them all'), shove halfpenny (a board game using coins sliding into channels on a polished wooden board) being used in one corner, darts in another and always so hot and airless—we never used it again.

Most schools were having problems with staff. Now so many male teachers were being called up to serve in the forces, many of the teachers were retired older people returning to fill in the gaps left as the young men left for war. Our local school also closed but on the opposite corner to our house stood a large Victorian building used by the local council. The top floor was converted and used as a temporary schoolroom. Local children like myself were sent there for half a day. It was quite nice except for gas mask drill. All the family had collected our gas masks from the local council office, black ones for Mum and Dad and me with an oval plastic window to see through. Breathing in was OK but breathing out produced a rude noise much to everyone's amusement. My sister Jean being a baby had a rubber cradle with a large window in it to see that the baby was not distressed, a pump was used to keep fresh air flowing through the filter.

I hated my mask, it frightened me to death as it covered my face when I was first made to wear it. So my mother told my school mistress about this problem, as we always had to carry our gas mask with us. She soon had us all doing gas mask drill in class, I soon found my fears had gone and we all enjoyed making rude noises together. In this class at the time was a boy named Jimmy Hughes, unbeknown to me at the time, we were soon to become lifelong friends.

Most people were now taking the war seriously enough to dig into their gardens, so-called Andersen Shelters, made from curved corrugate steel panels, half set in the ground, top covered with soil from the digging. Not bomb proof, but blast proof, big enough to take the whole family with bunk beds, an oil lamp, a chamber pot, flasks of tea, any spare food. Sounds just like camping doesn't it? Unfortunately they often filled up with water and were unusable, but although damp and cramped it was better than being blown apart in your house in a raid.

We were unable to build an Andersen Shelter, our garden by now was much reduced by Dad building a large garage opening onto the side street. He had plans to open a car hire business. With petrol rationing, cars privately owned would be a thing of the past, so his car sales was to close soon and Parsons Car Hire was about to be born. Remember self employed people have to adapt quickly.

So our air raid shelter was built by Dad in the basement of our house. Being below ground it was ideal, using huge timbers to hold up the floor above, with steel sheets above this—it was probably as safe as most shelters, unless there was a direct hit. No shelter was safe then, you would all be dead. Camp beds, candles, chamber pots, food, just in case the house blew down on top of us, and we would then have to wait to be dug out. So here we are, all set for the worst Hitler can do to us with nothing happening.

Life for me during this very quiet time was full of fun and new adventures. A regular visitor who I was always pleased to see was my grandfather, old Joe Parsons. Joe had his own business hauling flour to the bakers shops in town. One treat was for me to be taken out with him on his deliveries. He would collect me in the morning early, I would climb up onto the driver's seat very high above the horses, he would wrap a sack over my lap and off we would go. Very exciting—the clatter of the wheels on the cobbled streets, the smell of the horses, the horses' nosebag hanging on the back of the cart had a wonderful smell of oats and chaff.

'Do you want to drive?' Granddad would say after we had reached a quiet spot, handing me the reins. I took charge of two beautiful horses, "gee up" to start and "Wo" to stop. I never saw him use the whip on them ever although it was at hand, fixed into a whip holder on the side of the seat, black-plaited and shining with its silver decorations on the handle.

London was full of pubs at this time on every corner. Granddad loved his beer, and on his deliveries of flour to the many bakers on his round, there was also many pubs. So for every stop at a bakers he would stop at a pub. Amazingly Old Pole (that was the name of his favourite horse) would know just where and when to stop, no need to say "Wo". He just stopped outside each pub, waited for Granddad to strap on his nosebag with some hay in it, stand still as a statue, enjoying the stops as Granddad enjoyed his beer. I would be given a bag of crisps and a lemonade. So we all enjoyed the stops.

Half an hour later Granddad would emerge from the pub, face a little redder, filling his pipe with a sweet-smelling tobacco from his yellow tobacco pouch, a match is lit, masses of smoke billows from the pipe hanging from the side of his mouth. "Gee up Pole" and we were off. Again to the next bakers and of course the next pub. No problem ... Old Pole knew the way.

Now as I have said Granddad liked to drink. A very jolly man with a grey moustache that used to dip into his beer when he drank, leaving thick white froth to be wiped off with back of his hand, he also must have been a very difficult man to live with. My grandmother who died before I was born, was a very thrifty lady. Granddad was a boozer, on at least two occasions he sold his flour haulage business in the pub on a Saturday night for cash and in a drunken stupor disappeared for a number of weeks, taking with him his drinking mate and two old birds they had picked up that night.

He would arrive back home when the money was gone, spin Grandmother some tale, be forgiven, ask her for some money to buy a horse and cart to start up in business again. My father said she did this for him more than once. He must have been a smoothie chops to get away with it so often.

Grandmother always had that hoard of gold sovereigns tucked away and Granddad knew she would get him started again. When she died Granddad managed to get his hands on a very large amount of these sovereigns, never worked again until they were all gone—most of them over the bar of the Flying Dutchman Pub in Southampton Way, Camberwell. I often wondered where she got the sovereigns from, probably from his pocket when he was drunk, which was often.

One of his regular visits to the pub was made by donkey and cart and there was a reason for this, the cart was very low and the donkey knew its way home on its own. So on pub turning-out time Granddad Parsons would stagger to the cart, fall in the back, sometimes with a pal or two, say "Gee up" to the donkey which would gently take him home, stopping outside his house allowing him to stagger in.

My father said many times he would wake in the morning, look out of the window to see his dad still sound asleep in the cart. When he was able to walk to the house, he would often cook huge beefsteaks at 2am in the morning—the smell driving my father mad with hunger as it drifted up to his bedroom above.

I think he must have been a one for the ladies, old Joe Parsons. I remember when he was in his eighties he said he still liked women but was not sure if he could do it any more. He had our family in roars of laughter when he said, 'I would not mind a try, so if you lift me on I could roll off on my own'.

What an old rascal he was without any doubt, but such a character, old Joe. For sure he certainly enjoyed life. He told my father that he was born with nothing and he intended to die with nothing. Well, he certainly got his wish, his only problem being he was broke from fifty years old, but died at eighty four years—thirty years being quite hard up.

When he was in his seventies he would walk from Camberwell to Peckham to visit his son. Dad always gave him money on these occasions, which was spent in the pub on his way home. He lived with a lady and her spinster daughter Sara, his landlady Mrs Homiston, a big fat woman who smelt of sweat and moth balls, and was his bedmate for sure—but no one talked about things of a personal nature in those days.

I hated going to their home for visits, as I was always left with Aunt Sara while they all went off to the pub for a drink. I would watch the big ticking clock drag its hands round so slowly that they seemed hardly to move (still hate ticking clocks in the room to this day).

On her dining table was a large dish with wax fruit on it. I would stare at the fruit for hours, convinced that it must taste good and wishing I could take a bite. A large aspidistra plant completed the depressing scene, pure Victoriana interior. Very dark and very quiet except for that damn slow ticking clock. Aunt Sara would glare at me with her pale acne-pitted face if I so much as spoke or moved. She was really quite sad, never married, plain as a pike staff, living in a Cinderella-type of existence, totally under the dominance of her mother. So I am sure Aunt Sara hated these occasions when she was left to look after me, while they all went out for a gay old time at the pub.

One day in a moment of compassion Dad had decided it would be nice to buy Granddad a horse and trap—he felt sorry for him walking everywhere at his age. So off we all went to the Elephant and Castle Horse Auctions. Many horses were paraded that day, trotted up and down in front of the hopeful buyers. As the auctioneer called out for bids, one horse, a bay mare caught Dad's eye and after a few bids to the auctioneer she was ours.

Granddad had earlier looked at her teeth, and she moved well. She was a bit dirty but we would soon smarten her up. Now for the trap. These were sold in the afternoon after the horses were sold. Dad's hand swiped in the air again. The auctioneer knew Dad well and was sure Dad would give him a present of a few pounds if he was the successful bidder (not considered a bribe in those days). The hammer fell and the most lovely little black shining two-wheeled trap was ours. Later Dad bought a complete set of harness for the horse. Now Granddad was all set up with his own transport, and in some style I might add.

We saw quite a lot of him for some weeks after this, looking very snappy with his pipe billowing smoke as he shot off at quite a pace, for this was his version of a smart sports car. The black and shining trap, being very light, shot into the air as the mare dug her heels in.

Well, he certainly cut a dash for all of three months. Then

he sold the lot and spent the money in the pub as usual. Dad was very angry about this and Granddad kept his distance for quite a while.

1960. 121 Peckham Road awaiting demolition and in a neglected condition. My sister Jean in the foreground

CHAPTER FIVE

BOMBERS OVER LONDON

The phoney war period was still on, nothing happening for us to fear. Schools were talking of evacuation, mass bombing of our City was expected. Hitler had flattened cities in Poland and Spain. We were to be next, but so far nothing had happened. Then it did, being so young between six and seven years old, the first time I saw Hitler's might was in the air above.

We were sitting in the garden on a bright, clear sunny day, when the throb of aircraft engines could be heard in the distance—the deep throb of diesel motors quite different from our own aircraft engines. They used petrol and made a steady purring sound. We looked up over the rooftops, searching the sky. Then suddenly they burst into view, hundreds of them, jet black against the bright sky. In close formation, as far as we could see in any direction, were those dreaded bombers sent to destroy our city. They seemed so very low, twin-engined aircraft in perfect formation. There did not seem to be any air raid warning sounded.

We were completely unprepared. We were sure they

would just open their bomb doors and kill us all. I remember a lot of panic and I ngled and was very scared. To our amazement the large formation of bombers continued on their way. They were looking for more important targets than 121 Peckham Road. They hit the docks very hard that day causing tremendous damage to the Thameside warehouses and waterfront area. Hitler had a lot more to come yet, but to me this was the start of the war.

Well, we were in a war now, schools started sending children off to the country by the train load. If you see the old newsreels of the time they all seemed so happy. That was not so, children hated the idea and even more so did the parents, going to total strangers. Picked out like puppy dogs at the Village hall, a few left 'till last, not wanted and feeling homesick and rejected.

Mum decided not to send me, thank goodness. She felt I could go to stay with my Mum's sister, Aunt Daisy who lived in West Malling—hardly out of London, but away from the city centre, Hitler's main target of the time.

Aunt Daisy was a nice lady, always very smart in her dress, kept a perfect home smelling of wax polish and brass shining everywhere. Uncle Mick was kind, always had a problem with his back which meant that he walked with a stick and, later in his life, became quite handicapped and needed a serious operation as quite an old man. It appealed to me to go to Aunt Daisy's mainly because of her three daughters, the youngest called Irene, about one year older than me, blonde hair and very pretty. I found myself attracted to her. It's amazing how being so very young, my interest in the opposite sex showed itself, but it did. I was fascinated by her and was disappointed to hear cousins could not get married.

My stay with Aunt Daisy was quite short owing to a few

setbacks. One problem was that I had just found out that playing with one's little appendage between one's legs was rather nice. What I did not know at this age was that to do it in public was not nice. Well, one lunchtime I felt bored while sitting at the table and my hand wandered down to the spot on my body that I had started to find so entertaining. Probably having a glazed look on my face and the table cloth jumping about, it did not take long for my aunt to guess what I was up to.

'Stop that,' she snapped.

I complied and felt guilty. Now I knew if you do anything involving sex keep it to yourself, probably my first lesson in life.

My second problem was my cousin Irene. She seemed more interested in my little appendage than even I was. In my aunt's garden behind the rose bushes stood their Andersen shelter, half in the ground, the rest covered with earth—a smashing place to use as a camp. This was used by Irene and me as a perfect place to play cowboys and Indians, Mums and Dads and my favourite game, doctors and nurses.

In one of these doctors and nurses games, Irene decided to remove her knickers. I was fascinated with what I saw. She was very keen that I should investigate in true doctor style. I liked this game. Then she became very demanding. I was quite happy to show her my little appendage but she insisted I submerged the little fella in a glass of cold water that was standing on the nearby table. Even at this tender age I was never one to be a spoilsport so I obliged.

Well, all us chaps know that you don't get much fun doing something like that, perhaps it was the magnifying effect that fascinated her. To be fair, doing it once for her was fun, but then she demanded a repeat performance. I said no. She then said she would tell her Mum if I didn't. I burst into tears, ran out of the shelter into the kitchen and told my aunt what had happened.

Well, this was probably the last straw for Aunt Daisy, but more disaster was about to fall upon me. Whether out of fear and the interrogation that Aunt gave me, immediately after being sent to my room I had an urgent need to visit the toilet. Rushing up the many flights of stairs in a desperate attempt to beat nature's determination for me to disgrace myself on the spot, I at last made it to the door. But to my dismay nature had beaten me to it.

Oh, my god, what a mess to be in, in every sense. I did not feel this was a good time to mention this to my aunt, so I cleaned up as best as a six year old boy could do and, terrified as to what my aunt would say, I decided to keep quiet about the whole thing and hope to go undetected. I did not last very long. All the family kept sniffing the air with lots of 'Oh, god that awful smell.'

Needless to say, a few days later I was sent home in disgrace.

Coming home to Peckham was nice. The war, unbeknown to me, was probably in its 'Battle of Britain' stage—no night bombing, Hitler came over in daylight and was getting a bloody nose from our fighter aircraft. Life was going on as usual, except for rationing of food. We all had our own ration books that would be used to buy groceries at 'Len's Corner Shop'. Len was a lovely man, always jolly. His only son John became my lifelong friend. Opposite was a newsagent, 'Compton's' ... a regular visit on Mondays to buy 'The Beano' and 'Dandy' comics. I probably had the first editions, worth a fortune now.

The streets were very quiet, hardly any cars on the road. This meant that we boys could use the streets as our playground quite safely. On Compton's shop side wall we drew a wicket in chalk and our cricket pitch was down the centre of the road. We were very seldom disturbed by traffic needing to come past us.

It was so nice to be back home again with my friends. We were all now into plane spotting, becoming very excited if we saw a Spitfire fly over, we would wave and cheer at our heroes high above, how brave they were.

My grandmother, Nanny George, my mother's mother, was a wonderful kind warm lady, quite a big woman who lived at this time on One Tree Hill, near Peckham Rye. Granddad George was a stern-faced loud-voiced man who in World War One was blown out of his lorry by a shell and lived to tell the story. This happened at the famous hellfire corner, a spot where so many met their deaths in that terrible bloody war. He was very proud to have served his country in the 1914–18 war and would on any excuse show us grandchildren his campaign medals, always bright and shiny.

'They're yours on your eighteenth birthday,' he told me. He was so pleased that I was interested enough to want them. I have treasured them all my life. He would be very pleased that I have kept them for future generations of our family to see.

Granddad worked for London Transport. His job was to service the trams that screamed around the London main roads ... noisy, clanking, trams running a few yards from our house day and night. Amazingly after a few weeks we did not notice them any more, never, even at night. The conductors on these trams were by now all women. We called them 'clippies', the reason being their punch machines that made a small hole in your ticket giving a delightful little ding as the hole was punched in. Getting onto a tram was a risky business. The tram stopped in the middle of the road, passengers getting on or off had to beware of traffic as they tried to reach the pavement. As the roads were very quiet accidents were very rare.

Peckham had three cinemas, the Odeon in Peckham Road, a very smart dream world that we could visit once a week to see the latest films, mostly from Hollywood. We would go early about 6pm to miss the large queues that formed for the late show at 7ish. We always saw the end of the main film first and as there were always two film shows, we would always leave the cinema in the middle of the main feature. Dad would jump up declaring, 'Well, this is where we came in.' Out we would go, knowing the end of the film before we saw the beginning. It did not seem the least bit strange at the time.

I suppose the adventure of going to the cinema was the exciting part. Often when watching a film the screen would show a notice saying that an air raid warning had been sounded outside. Very few people would leave the theatre. I suppose we felt quite safe sitting in the dark, our minds dreamily involved in the glamour and happiness being portrayed on the large silver screen in front of us.

Of the other two cinemas, The Tower in Rye Lane was equally grand, an old variety theatre converted when films came along. The Gaumont Cinema near Queens Road was our third choice. In one week we visited all three.

Without fail every week of the year, rain or shine, winter or summer—plus, for children, Saturday morning children only show. These were great, all full of screaming kids throwing things at each other, no grown-ups anywhere, the attendants did their best to control us. But this was our magic worlds of Flash Gordon adventures, Hoppalong Cassidy, Adventures of Rin Tin Tin, A Well Trained Dog.

We sang songs following a bouncing ball on a song sheet up on the silver screen, oh how we loved the cinema.

We loved it so much that bunking in was a pastime with us boys. We would gather outside the exit doors on a Saturday afternoon, having earlier acquired a short piece of bailing wire. This was inserted in the gap in the door, having shaped the wire into a hook. All that was needed was to connect with the emergency bar on the inside of the door. One sharp tug and the door flew open for us.

Now came the tricky part. We all drew straws as to who went first, because once inside we had to avoid the attendants. They knew our little game and the first kid up front would possibly get caught if things went wrong. The time I was unfortunate enough to go first, things went very wrong for me.

Being the first of about ten boys creeping up the stairs at the Gaumont Cinema, on my hands and knees, I opened the door to the inside of the theatre, pushing my head through first, my body almost flat on the floor.

I had just got my head and shoulders through the door, leaving a tell-tale crack of light piercing the darkness inside. Bang! An explosion erupted in my head. I spun round seeking escape. The attendant had been waiting on the inside of the door and had delivered a mighty blow to my head with his torch. In total panic we all fled down the staircase, falling over ourselves to avoid the grab on the neck by the attendant that meant capture and a good whacking to the head as well.

On my flight down the stairs I was determined not to be last. The flight of panic was accompanied by a warm wet feeling in my baggy underpants that always seemed to hang down below my short trousers. Yes, I had peed myself with fear. Fortunately they had dried by the time I got home so my crime went undetected.

CHAPTER SIX

BATTLE OF BRITAIN

September 1940 was a turning point for the British. Hitler had tried to destroy us in the air before attempting an invasion by sea. This little Briton had a front row seat as the sky over Kent became a battleground to stop the Nazi war machine.

My grandmother loved to go hop picking as a paid holiday in the hop fields of Kent. 'Hopping', we called it. Large numbers of Londoners travelled down to Kent every year to bring in the hop harvest, living in tin huts, just one room situated on the farmer's land. It must sound quite primitive to live in one room, to cook on an open wood fire just outside the hut, to get your drinking water from a central tap in cans, to be given a bundle of wood called a fagot to use as fuel to cook on, and straw was provided to stuff our mattress.

We had arrived by train at Goudhurst Station, everything we needed in suitcases piled on to my aunt's pram. We must have looked like refugees wheeling this pram with our bundles on top, down the hill to Spelmondon Farm, bouncing our squeaking pram containing my little cousin Johnny Robins hardly visible below the bundle and bags—as my Aunt Nance, Nan and me weaved our way down the farmer's rutted road.

At the end of this track a large field came into view, surrounded by black-painted tin huts much like garden sheds, all in a line, each with its own number on the door. A small window allowed a bright shaft of light to pierce through the otherwise dark interior where we found a room some 15ft x 15ft. At one end was a wooden platform raised above the floor by about 2ft and slatted, on this platform stood a large bale of straw. There were no cupboards or shelves, just whitewashed corrugated iron walls on a concrete floor.

Our first job was to unpack our suitcases. Under the wooden platform, soon to become our bed, went anything not needed there and then. Sheets had previously been sewn together to form a giant pillow case. Busting open the bale of straw, we stuffed handfuls into the sheets until the whole thing was now a very crunchy-sounding mattress. After adding sheets pillows and blankets, a very large and surprisingly comfortable bed appeared, plenty big enough for our small family. Other huts would house huge families with countless children, for this was a working holiday for poor people, remember.

Outside each hut lay a little bundle of wood tied together with thick twine, the farmer's fagot! Bone dry and ready to burn, we soon had our campfire going. Tripods were made from the larger sticks to suspend pots bubbling with stews in them, big soot-blacked kettles pushed deep into the glowing embers whistled away merrily, ready for endless cups of tea. Potatoes baking on stones placed nearby, plates knives and forks at the ready—we all sat round our fires talking excitedly and by now starving. The smell of the food cooking on an open fire was wonderful, it was difficult to keep our mouths from overflowing.

The first meal over and after sitting around our camp enjoying the night sky and feeling the heat on our faces it was time for bed. Diving into the straw-filled mattress was fun. Nan, Aunt, baby Johnny and me all snuggled down together. Being too excited to sleep, Aunt Nance, my favourite aunt, agreed to tell some stories. Aunt Nance being only about twenty five years old herself, the youngest of three daughters, had a wild streak in her that I was attracted to. She seemed to be on our level more than other adults in the family. When I was older she would encourage me to 'hop the wag', a term for not arriving at school, so she could take me to the pictures instead.

I liked her, she was rebellious, she also had a tendency to steal but this came later. Her stories told that night were hair-curling, she was wonderfully descriptive, describing the new films she had seen at the cinema. Frankenstein's Monster, The Curse of the Mummy, all with the actor Boris Karloff playing the lead—these were the horror films of the 1930s. Trying to go to sleep after these stories was very hard with the oil lamp flicking shadows on the walls, each one looking like a monster.

Next morning we were up at 6am. There was a sharp chill in the bright September sunlight, our little band of lookalike refugees following the pole pullers and binmen into the hopfields some short walk from our little tin huts. Here we were given our hop bins, an odd-shaped sack container with poles to lift, much like a stretcher. As we moved down the avenue of hop vines, the pole pullers followed the hop picker to remove the hop vines that became broken off at the top of the very high supporting strings. The vines as they grew, twisting their way to the sunlight above, became impossible for us to reach, so he had a very long pole with a cutting edge that cut them down for us. The pole puller wore a poke on his head, a sack shaped like hood that was worn to keep the very wet falling vines from falling onto him. Have you ever heard the saying 'don't buy a pig in a poke'? The poke being the sack, the moral is, be sure of what you are buying.

The bin men would move through the rows of pickers, removing hops from the bins, using a large basket called a bushel measure. The amount collected would be recorded in Nan's picker's book and at the end of our stay she would be paid for her work by the bushel. So it was a holiday away from the sooty grime of London and you took home money as well. Aunt Nance would receive her share and even I was given some pocket money as a reward for picking the odd hop.

As in most childhood memories, the day away seemed hot and sunny and I soon became bored with picking hops—and more enjoyed the freedom and friendship found with the other boys than staying with Nan and Aunt. Most days our gang of about five or six boys aged from seven to ten years of age would fish, make camps in the woods, play Robin Hood, bake potatoes in campfires. Total freedom unheard of today—children were completely safe, it really was a happy time.

The villagers at Goudhurst really hated the hop pickers descending on them every year in September. Must have been a nightmare, drunk and noisy in the pubs, stealing everywhere, it became so bad that the grocer shops would wire in their goods and only serve us through a small hatch for fear of shoplifting. As the farm was at the very bottom of Goudhurst Hill, every item we needed involved a long trek uphill to Goudhurst Village centre, so you can imagine this band of lookalike gypsies with their prams and pushchairs, muddy clothes and wellingtons contaminating their very pretty village.

Real life gypsies were regular pickers for the farmers. Totally unlike today's gypsies, these people lived in their own very brightly painted horsedrawn Romany caravans, highly decorated in reds and yellows. When not picking hops they would be seen sitting round their fires cutting clothes pegs from hazel twigs, these they sold from door to door. This gypsy, the true gypsy was as one with his environment. They were respected by all. They wore brightly coloured clothes, bandannas on their heads, very much like their Spanish forefathers.

Back at the farm my Aunt Nance would return early before picking had ended to enable her to start our campfire and prepare the evening meal. This must have been quite hard for her as her little boy, my cousin Johnny, was quite young. Arriving home to a hot meal, sitting around the campfire was the highlight of the day.

As is nature's calling after meals, it meant a visit to the camp toilet. This was a very horrible experience. Some way beyond the camp would be a series of wooden huts neatly in a row. On entering a revolting stench hit the nostrils and your face was bombarded with blue bottles trying to get out as you came in. When your eyes adjusted to the half light, before you stood the toilet, you would see a wooden box with one, or sometimes two toilet seat holes side by side in case you went with a friend, suspended over a quite deep hole in the ground—usually nearly full with human excrement, when full the hole would be filled in and the hut moved to a new spot nearby.

Well, I could not stomach this stink, so a quick visit to the woods was the way to avoid these vile little huts, a large leaf as toilet paper and don't sit on the stinging nettles.

Every day seemed sunny and warm. This was a very nice September, nice for us working in the fields in Kent, the Garden of England. Skies were clear blue, but not peaceful. For this was September 1940, our land was ours, but in our skies the black cross and swastika was to be seen, Hitler's evil Nazis wanted to enslave us, and our young men would fight and, oh so often, die in these beautiful blue skies, so bravely in their Hurricanes and Spitfires. They were my heroes. How I would have loved to be a dashing RAF flyer with wings on my uniform, my own Spitfire, to be admired, to save my country, to be a hero.

But at seven years old I had to be content to fantasise myself into their lives. This was done by learning all I could about aircraft. I knew every aircraft by its silhouette shape, could tell you its speed and firepower, how many crew were needed. This was common knowledge with all us boys, we would test each other using black silhouette cutouts of aircraft held above our head against the blue sky.

There was nothing that we did not know about the RAF, especially fighters. The words still thrill me, Spitfire, Hurricane ... our answer to the black shapes flying in total arrogance in our skies, determined to crush us into submission. Can you imagine what it was like—the enemy is here, in your country, intent on taking by force everything you hold dear, to kill, rape, loot, destroy, plunder, as they had already done all over Europe. Feel anger? Deep blood boiling anger?

Well, that's how we all felt but anger was not enough. Our young men had to face horrible death in these blue skies high above the fields in which one little boy looked up with so much admiration.

They seemed like small black dots, enemy aircraft flying very high in tight formation. There they are, came shouts from all around heads bent back as eyes shielded by palms of hands searched the clear sky, twenty, thirty, sixty, possibly a hundred of black dots appeared too high to see the dreaded black crosses.

But they were bombers alright, we had nothing to fear, Hitler's might was out for a bigger prize than our little helpless group. LONDON—almost within bombing range by now only a few minutes away.

German air crew would be working hard at last minute checks, bomb aimers in position, navigator checking correct bombing runs to target area, probably London Docks. They seemed all set for a successful raid once again, but this was not to be so easy this time. Among the black dots there now appeared small white streaks in the sky, they seemed to be even higher than the German aircraft.

By this time all hop picking had stopped, people were all totally fascinated by the real life drama unfolding in front of them, some now lying on their backs staring into the bright sky. Fighters from fighter command had attacked the formation, it was impossible to tell from far below how successful our boys were doing, but the white streaks from their vapour trails told their own story.

They were attacking from high above the German formations. If possible we always attacked from out of the sun and high above, making it impossible for the German gun crews to see an attacking Spitfire with the sun in their eyes. They had been lying in wait, alerted by radar, long before the raiders had crossed our coast. I can imagine the shock for the crews hearing the first screams over the intercoms … 'auchtung, Spitfire' … as our aircraft with eight machine guns firing, scythed through their formations.

If I sound heartless you are right. As I write this I still remember how much I hated the Germans. We wanted them dead, these were a vicious cruel enemy. The vapour trails seemed to go round in circles until the whole sky became like a crazily woven basket, white streaks everywhere. Far above the muffled chatter of machine guns could be heard as this deadly fight for survival unfolded.

The formation seemed to breakup. In the distance planes falling to the ground, smoke pouring from their engines, impossible for us to know whether we should cheer or cry at that distance, it was just an aircraft. In every direction little white balloons seemed to appear falling slowly to earth.

We all watched in silence, no sound in the sky above ... JUST SILENCE ... the tiny balloons now visible as parachutes, with their very lucky aircrews gently, oh so very gently, floating down to the fields below. How many died a blazing death that day only records would show. I do know that for one young man it was for him and for us a day to be proud of.

In the distance at very low treetop height it came roaring straight at us ... Was this an embittered German escort fighter intending to revenge himself for their failed raid on these helpless civilians below? As we ducked down out of fear, the fighter rolled his aircraft, wings nearly touching the tops of our hop vines. It was a Spitfire in full camouflage colouring doing a victory roll. A complete rotation of an aircraft at low level was called a victory roll, denoting a kill—forbidden by Commanders, as after battle things had the nasty habit of falling off, but this young man was ecstatic and wanted our approval.

Boy, did we approve! We cheered and cheered. All of us hoping he might hear above the deep-throated roar of his 12-cylinder Rolls Royce Merlin engine. Of course he would hear nothing in the confines of his cockpit but we would have seen the ecstatic waving from the fields below, waving and cheering him safely home.

He gave us all a farewell wave with his wings, all over in seconds but remembered by one little boy with admiration for life.

Early next morning the bright sun tried hard to shine through the heavy mist surrounding Spelmondon Farm.

Rumours that an enemy aircraft had crashed on the hill above the farm, quickly had us boys heading in that direction, following the narrow winding road in the direction of Goudhurst Village. Nothing was seen until halfway up the hill, then to the right beyond a small copse, the figures of two Home Guard Soldiers could be seen, their ill-fitting uniforms and grey hair making it obvious that these men were part of the famous Dad's Army.

Much to our dismay they were standing guard with rifles in hand, over not a Nazi bomber, but a Hurricane fighter. The aircraft had crash-landed in the meadow. Its rudder and fuselage riddled with bullet holes, the pilot with great skill and even greater luck had avoided the copse and safely landed his crippled fighter.

Being completely unhurt, he was able to once again walk away from a near brush with death. No doubt after a short drive to his squadron, the next day would find him sitting in a replacement Hurricane, flying in to attack the Nazi formations once again, high in the skies over Kent. England demanded bravery such as this from her young men in 1940 and she was not disappointed.

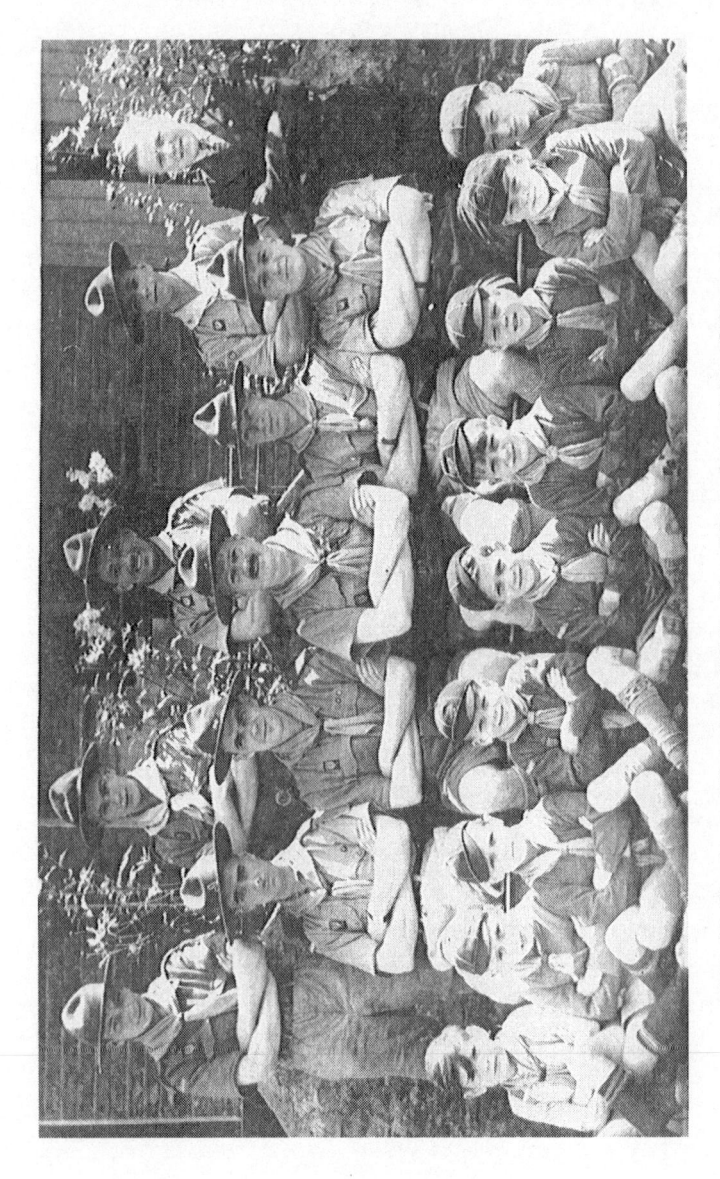

1940. 6th Camberwell Scouts and Cubs. The old war horse, Major Watson, centre. Freddie third from right, front row.

CHAPTER SEVEN

EVACUATION

Returning home from my hop picking adventure, Peckham seemed a little tame. School had become rather irregular owing to teacher shortage. That pleased me as I hated school anyway. The bombing had become more intense, Hitler using the cover of darkness to try to achieve at night what he had failed during the daylight hours.

Huddled in our shelter every night, hearing the screams as the bombs fell, the thunderous explosion as high explosives rained all around, the throb, throb, of the German aircraft diesel engines high above as the searchlights pierce the blackness hoping to find them.

Each night must have been a nightmare for my Mum and Dad. We children saw no danger and would sleep through all but the very noisy raids. Every day saw more damage, whole streets would disappear into a pile of bricks and broken timber, police and air raid wardens, working to find families trapped under tons of debris. It was probably sights like these that prompted Mum and Dad's decision to try to leave London at nights to avoid some of the bombing.

Dad's car hire business was going along quite well, lots

of servicemen needing transport to and from the railway stations in London. Having only one large car seating seven people he was kept very busy most of the time. One of his friends, a successful motor parts dealer Harry Northwood, was making regular trips to Epsom Downs staying in and sleeping on the floor of some golf huts at the rear of the Derby Arms public house opposite the grandstand of Epsom race course.

It was decided a rest from the bombing would do us all a lot of good, so one night loading his car with four neighbours and ourselves we set out for Epsom, leaving in daylight as the bombers never attacked until dusk. Arriving at Epsom Downs being shown to our hut to be shared with a very jolly man Mr Northwood and his family, we quickly made ourselves comfortable, mattress on the floor, an old oil heater to boil a kettle for tea in the morning. Once again I felt it was like camping, the pub completely surrounded by fields and open grassland was perfect for playing.

In the evening the grown ups drifted to the bars. We children played around outside with the usual glass of lemonade and a packet of crisps. It stayed light until very late, the change of two hours in the clocks kept the evenings light until 11pm. It some how helped with the bombing, being so regular. On some occasions Dad and I would sleep in his car, this made a comfortable double bed using the front seats to fill in the gaps. The car was parked near the golf huts and overlooking London. Being on high ground the view was perfect to see the searchlights and anti-aircraft gunfire lighting the sky up like a firework show. We would watch until tired, go to sleep glad we were out of it for one night at least.

We made the trip to Epsom on quite a regular basis for

quite some time, each night by a different route though. Because it was against the law for Dad to go outside a ten-mile radius of his garage, he would have been charged with wasting petrol and in wartime this would have been serious.

Epsom was sixteen miles from Peckham so the last six miles was a very anxious time. On one of these trips we left rather late and by the time we were half way there the bombers were overhead, the air raid sirens were singing their familiar wail. Travelling as fast as Dad's 1936 18hp saloon would go we shot along the Sutton by-pass, all hanging onto each other, scared stiff as the bombs began to fall. To be caught out in the open with steel fragments of shrapnel falling everywhere from our own gunfire, the bombers shedding their deadly load at the same time, meant we would be lucky to drive through it.

'Pull up,' said Mum. 'We should stop and take shelter.'

Slowing down Dad stopped under a bridge spanning the new Sutton by-pass, a nice new strong concrete bridge spanning the smart new motorway type by-pass.

We stopped for just a minute before Dad said, 'I'm not stopping here.'

He started the car, into gear and with the slow grinding acceleration of a 1936 car we sped on. Returning the next morning, to our shock and amazement, the bridge we had sheltered under was completely bombed away. A double-decker bus was standing on its end against the embankment. The bridge must have been a direct hit. If Dad had not moved on when he did I doubt if I would be telling you this story.

A few weeks later, arriving back to Peckham early in the morning after a very bad raid on London the night before, we were stopped by a police cordon across the road to our house.

'Can't go down there, mate,' said the steel-helmeted police officer. 'Unexploded bomb.'

Explaining that our house was quite near the white tapes across the road in front of us, the policeman agreed to let us through. As we drove closer to our house we were stunned to see how close a bomb had dropped. A huge tree on the opposite corner to our house was no longer there. In its place was a deep hole, debris was all over the road, all our windows had been blown in, a crack had appeared in the front of the house. The blast must have been fierce, but this was a small bomb otherwise every house for 100 yards around would have ceased to exist.

Stumbling over bricks, glass and what was left of the large tree, we put the key in our front door.

Dad then froze. 'Don't move,' he whispered.

Looking to our left below our basement front window, our eyes fell onto a large round orange steel cylinder, larger than a football, stuck into the ground and half covered with soil.

Oh, my god, it must have been the unexploded bomb. Beating a hasty retreat back to the white tapes and the police, we informed them of our find.

'Stay where you are,' said the head air raid warden.

A group of uniformed men moved very cautiously towards our house. A few moments of total silence, then peals of laughter broke out as they returned, tossing from one to another the orange ball that turned out to be the top of a zebra crossing beacon that used to stand near our house before the bomb had blown it all away. A very funny incident we all enjoyed with much relief.

Epsom Racecourse had a huge grandstand that was used during the war as barracks for Welsh Guards. The Derby Arms pub being opposite their barracks they were frequent visitors. Tall, handsome, very smart in their khaki uniforms with peak caps so flat it touched their noses, their cap badge a leak polished like burnished gold completed the overall picture of one of Britain's crack fighting regiments. They were very popular in the pub. We were extra nice to our boys, who at any time might be called upon to die for us all. Slaps on the back and free drinks was normal when they entered the bar.

We became especially friendly with one young Welshman, who said his mother owned a farm in Carmarthen ... and if Mum and Dad were worried about the bombing they could always send me to her home to stay. He was so nice, he took me for visits to the army barracks, met his friends (important to point out he was quite normal).

So it was decided to send me to Wales. Evacuation was normal procedure for children. To be sent to a farm would be extra nice for me. I don't remember obecting too much about going until I found myself one morning being taken to a railway station with a parcel label tied to my lapel with my name and destination on it.

The moment I was handed over to the train guard, sat down on a wooden box with all the luggage and odd cargo in the guards van—for I was sent 'Care of the Guard', a term used at the time to transport children by train—I panicked. The fear and despair I felt then was so strong I can still feel it fifty two years later.

The miserable journey to Wales took all day, arriving quite late at night. I was met by a group of strangers, who could not pacify this crying distressed seven year old. Sent to bed in some strange house surrounded by unfamiliar sights made it impossible to sleep that night. In the morning the full disappointment became aware to me.

The so-called farm was a terraced house in a back street slum. There was no electricity, only oil lamps, no indoor plumbing. We all washed under a long-handled iron pump in the backyard which meant you only splashed your face with cold water—on a cold morning that was brave enough. Inside the house it was filthy. Furniture with the stuffing falling out, springs poking through the seats of the chairs, very dark inside as there were only very small windows, smelt awful.

The family consisted of two small boys, one girl, all about my age, husband and wife and their lodger in whose bed I slept on my first night there as he was away at the time. From then onwards I slept four to a bed with the other children, all in a large double bed, toes to the middle—called top and toeing, quite common in poor overcrowded homes. The nearest this place got to looking like a farm was the few scrawny chickens they kept in the yard at the back of the house.

There was one other member of the family who terrified me, the old grandmother. I never saw her move from the large Windsor chair she occupied very close to the open fire in the kitchen-cum-living room. Scraggly grey hair and to me witchlike, she sat huddled over the fire and never ever spoke to me. Near her side was a stout walking stick and if you were foolish enough to get too close to her, she would swing the stick at you, cursing and muttering obscenities, probably in Welsh. What type of madhouse had I been sent to?

The local school was quite nice, a typical Victorian school, quite small and, being the only English boy there, I was soon speaking with a Welsh accent. I could 'look you die bark' as good as the rest of them, sing songs like 'sause bon vark a merry and a ta', a very well known Welsh song that I still remember the words to today.

Carmarthen Town Centre had a very large cattle market that we children enjoyed to visit on sale days, milling around the cattle pens had some interesting perks. The cattle men would milk a cow in front of us boys and hand round cups of blood-heat milk, thick with yellow cream on the top, which we would all drink down with great relish. Sounds revolting to me now, but was a great treat then.

Saturday morning was also very exciting. A visit to the local fleepit cinema to see, 'Flash Gordon's Adventures in Mars'. By this time the flees were not only in the cinema but had taken up residence on me—scratching had become a pastime. I was not aware that I had them, only that once a week the lady would go through my hair with a special comb to remove—as she called them—'bits of fluff'. All the other kids had 'bits of fluff' and I expect the whole house was full of 'bits of fluff'.

I had been living in Wales for over two months by now and had never changed my underclothes or had a bath ever. Mother had been sending money and clothes to these people regularly but I never saw anything. Whether by chance, or Mum was missing me by now, it was arranged that my parents should telephone me at the local police station.

I arrived at the pre-arranged time with my keepers, a short wait as the policeman on duty waited for our call to ring on his large black telephone. At home we had a similar large black telephone sitting on our front-room table, on the white disc in the centre of the dial was the number Rodney 4765 as each part of London was known by a name then a number.

At last the phone rang, breaking the silence that made me jump with excitement.

'Hello,' Mum said.

I was nearly crying with pleasure to hear her voice again after so long.

'How are you?' she said. 'Do you like it there? Do you miss us all?'

All these questions I was dying to answer with, I hate it and I want to come home. Instead I looked at my keepers' stern faces and answered, 'Yes I like it here, they are nice to me.'

I think they must have heard the lump in my throat as I hastily described my happiness.

On the way back to their house my keepers told me, 'Your Mum is coming down to see you soon.'

What a change in their attitude to me. I was given clean clothes, my hair was cut, but no bath, just a good wipe over with a flannel. The other children had their own pet puppy, a sweet little black and white mixed breed that I loved very much, but was told by the other children in a spiteful way, as children can be to each other, it's our puppy, not yours.

Imagine my amazement when the lady dropped this puppy into my lap, saying, 'He's yours now.'

I was over the moon. He's mine all mine. I sat and cuddled him for some time, the other two children glowering at me. They delightedly told me later that I would not be allowed to keep him, their mother only wanted to cheer me up. In fact two days later I was told the dog wasn't mine any more.

It was exactly three months after I had left home, that my Mum and Dad came to visit me in Wales, arriving by train. I jumped with joy to see them, it had been arranged that they should stay overnight with the family. To create a good impression with my parents, my keepers' eldest daughter, who I do not remember living with us, being about to get married, possessed all new bedding, including a beautiful eiderdown bedspread. So my keeper raided her bottom drawer, laid out their own bedroom with all this new linen to impress my family.

Mum and Dad saw through all this special treatment. The absolute squalor all around them was enough to convince them of their mistake. Why they trusted the word of a soldier they hardly knew, why they never came down to Wales to see for themselves before leaving me, I will never know. I can only feel that in that war so many children were going off to strangers with the schools evacuating thousands, that they did not fear for me.

The next day all three of us were sitting in the train going home. That feeling going home, going home, going home ... the most wonderful feeling in the world.

Sitting in the carriage as the powerful steam locomotive sped toward London and home, I started to get the itch, the bits of fluff were on the move again.

'Why are you scratching?' mother enquired.

'Oh, it's nothing ... it's only bits of fluff. The lady picks then out of my hair for me every week.'

My mother shot out of her seat, bent my head over her lap, and fingers started to spread my hair apart. She nearly died of shock, the flees scattered everywhere, slowly followed by grey crablike body lice. My mother told this story many times and apparently the flees and lice where so crowded they were crawling over each other. I was literally running alive with them, no wonder I scratched a bit.

All my life after this, if away from home, I would get a feeling of despair so strong that it would take all my willpower not to turn my car around and drive home. When I moved house, I yearned for my old home for months after moving. In the first year of being married, I would drive home eighteen miles every night to Peckham because I felt homesick. Only a little self analysis is needed to enable me to understand why.

CHAPTER EIGHT

DAD'S BLACK MARKET

Bombing in London was still very bad, our house was very lucky to be standing. In every direction around us were open areas, only a pile of bricks to mark the spot where homes had once been. Hitler was trying to break our moral by blanket-bombing civilian areas night after night. He completely failed to do this. The people were never so friendly as at this time, always joking, never downhearted. Food was meagre, but I was never hungry, ever.

Probably part of the reason I was never hungry was that Dad, as he was exempt from military service owing to having a gastric ulcer—that bled at the most convenient time just before his medical examination, and he was in Dulwich Hospital for a few weeks on ice only, to stop the bleeding—had to do fire watching as his contribution to the war effort.

A fire watcher had to patrol the factory or warehouse. If a fire bomb came through the roof he would extinguish the fire using a bucket of water and a short hose connected to a hand pump clipped to the side of the bucket. My Dad was a very small man, his steel helmet was quite large, and if he ran it wobbled from side to side. The sight of my Dad all set to put out the Great Fire of London was very comical. When Dad later found out that these fire bombs now exploded after a time delay, he felt that watching would be the only part of his job he was prepared to do.

A large warehouse at the rear of Tankard & Smiths Garage was his allocated fire-watcher's location. This was on the corner of Camden Grove, only the next street to our own, so just a short walk for him and his bucket. It was extra convenient for him, as by now his fleet of cars also included two 1938 Humber Pullman Saloons that he garaged at night under the very large concrete forecourt canopy that covered the tall petrol pumps that stood outside the garage. This protected his cars from shrapnel that would fall during the heavy anti aircraft gunfire put up every night in the raids.

To give my Dad the keys to the warehouse at night and to leave him all alone with the contents must have made him grin from ear to ear. Opening the large green sliding door was a sight to behold. As far as you could see ... food, boxes and boxes. Opening other doors to find himself standing in cold-storage rooms with hundreds of carcasses of sheep, pigs, beef, all hanging in rows, covered with white muslin cloths ready to be distributed to London butcher shops. For this was a meat distribution centre and my Dad was in charge of it all, for all night. Boy, would he do some re-distribution!

The next morning there was the smell of kidneys sizzling in the frying pan to greet us all at breakfast. From there on it was quite common for us to have kidneys, as these could be cut out of the sheep carcasses and go unnoticed by the meat checkers. Dad became quite friendly with many of the meat porters working in the warehouse, big strong chaps in bloody white coats, carrying half a side of beef over their shoulders, tossing them into the delivery vans with so little effort.

Well, sometimes these chaps would make a detour in the direction of my Dad's cars parked just behind the petrol pumps.

'One in the back, Fred', given with a smile and a wink as they walked past.

That night we would be hacking a sheep carcass into joints on the kitchen table, using choppers and hacksaws until it disappeared into small bags to be distributed round all our family and friends. We never sold food to make a profit, just enough to cover the cash paid to the meat porter.

Petrol being on ration, there was always a black market in urgent need of a supply. Dad, being very resourceful, accepted—reluctantly, of course—the job of petrol pump attendant. He very quickly found an angle to his advantage. Petrol was only sold if you had a coupon. No coupon, no petrol. The one exception to this was the fire brigade and ambulance vehicles.

All manner of small vans and trucks were converted to service use at the outbreak of war. These chaps would fill their tanks to the full every day. Did I say to the full? Well, nearly to the full would be more to the truth. The odd gallon or so would be left still in the pumps, the driver would sign to say he was full, the usual few bob was dropped in his outstretched hand and at the end of the day all those extra gallons left over were Dad's. Only one problem, this petrol had red dye in it. The police had a way they could test your tank if you were ever stopped by them—if you had red petrol you really were in trouble.

The bartering that went on at this time was unbelievable. Dad would exchange his legally-obtained petrol coupons for sweets, also on ration, from Mr Beckett who owned the confectionery shop opposite us in Peckham Road. Dad could not exchange the red petrol for chocolate because Mr Beckett was also a policeman—even Dad could not go that far.

On one occasion our kitchen cabinet was full of massive bars of cooking chocolate that Dad had exchanged for tinned corned beef that had lost its way from the meat warehouse. At the end of the war when the final check was made on the warehouse contents, all the crates containing corned beef were full of house bricks instead. How many Dad placed there no one will ever know. I enjoyed the chocolate. Being large bars, I could break bits off and it would go unnoticed.

Stories about my Dad are quite hilarious but he was not a hilarious person. I never heard him tell a joke, he disliked company. At Christmas he would come down with gastric attacks to avoid joining in the Christmas fun. Most times at Christmas he would sit in a corner of the room and avoid everyone. When he did decide to become sociable he would talk so much people could not get away from him. The amazing thing about relating Dad's stories is they all seem so unbelievable. He had a totally unappealing nature and was totally disinterested in anyone but himself, yet he was outrageous. Looking back, even I cannot help but see the funny side of him.

An example was the many times he would stack four or five bars of tempting milk chocolate he had been given by his friend Mr Beckett on the corner of the mantelpiece in full view of my sister Jean and myself, knowing full well we had no sweets ourselves. The sight of all this chocolate, so temptingly close, drove us to desperation. So we would wait till he was out of the room and with a quick look over our shoulders steal a square—never more than one square—gobble it down quickly, hoping he would not notice. He would check his hoard of chocolate on a regular basis, square by square, and would go mad if one was missing. Why he never kept them out of sight from us I will never know. I think he was so insensitive that it never occurred to him.

Fire-watcher Dad, when on duty at the warehouse, would check all was well, and after removing next morning's breakfast from the sheep, would often sit with a friend or two on a low wall close to the petrol pumps, passing the long night away with cigarette and a nice chat. Protected by the large concrete canopy that covered the forecourt area, even at the height of an air raid, they would sit there and watch the searchlights picking out bombers in their beams. Bombs falling all around, they became used to the danger, and after all, a fire watcher could not take cover in a raid. His job was to note where a fire bomb had dropped and if possible extinguish it before a serious fire took hold.

Dad always said it was better to be born lucky than rich. Well, he certainly was lucky all his life and that luck was with him one night. After sitting on that wall for weeks and weeks, the night he was off duty, a fierce raid started about midnight. Our anti-aircraft guns blazed away into the black night, putting up a deafening barrage.

Knock knock, hammered on our door. All the family were deep in the cellar for safety. Dad rushed up the narrow stairs opening the door to a white-faced warden.

'Come quickly, Fred,' he said. 'Your car's a wreck. Bring some shovels, there is petrol everywhere.'

The sight that met Dad's eyes in the half dark must have made him want to cry. His big black Humber cars were full of holes—every window was smashed, every tyre ripped and flat—it was impossible to put a foot ruler between the holes. Petrol was pouring from the shattered tanks, soaking the forecourt with fuel that could be ignited at any moment by a careless act.

Under the forecourt in the petrol pump storage tank were countless thousands of gallons, one spark and the explosion would be heard for miles. Yet this was nothing to the sad sight at the base of the wall that was Dad's favourite spot when he was on duty.

An old tarpaulin sheet covered what was left of the two young men that were caught in the air raid and sadly took shelter under the canopy of the garage. An unexploded anti-aircraft shell had fallen to earth and exploded close to the wall where Dad would have been sitting. A hole in the hard concrete forecourt splintered by starburst gauges denoting the direction the thousands of steel fragments had taken, killing the two men outright, before ripping through Dad's cars.

There were bloodstains there for days afterwards and nobody sat on that wall ever again.

Within weeks Dad's cars had been repaired and resprayed like new. Only the odd tear in the neatly stitched-up head lining was left to tell the tale.

Site of Tankard and Smith's garage, now Kwik Fit. Passersby unaware that in the 1940s two men died as they sheltered from the air raid that would have killed Dad on any other night

CHAPTER NINE

REGMA OF LANGLEY BOTTOM

The trips down to Epsom had become quite regular again, owing to the raids making it very hard to get any sleep at night. At least when on Epsom Downs, it would be very bad luck indeed to have a bomb fall on you. This is where a very special lady comes into my story, a Mrs Sarah Ash. A happy friendly plumpish lady with short grey hair cut in a bob style, Mrs Ash lived in a detached house called 'Regma'. Her husband was Reg but she was always called Ma, not too fashionable today, but homely then to use such names.

They lived in Langley Bottom a mile or so from the Derby Arms Pub where Mum and Dad spent so many nice evenings. My first impression of Mrs Ash was when she entered the Derby Arms one night. I saw her dressed in full air-raid warden's uniform, blue boiler suit, steel helmet with a large white W on the front, stirrup pump at the ready, and all the equipment needed to put out the Great Fire of London.

The bar full of people who knew her well roared with laughter—this quite elderly lady ready to take on Hitler's might rather depicts the spirit that prevailed at this time.

Children were allowed in the bar provided they were very quiet, so I often slipped in to see and hear singing of wartime songs like 'Bless them all'. I loved to get to the line that said 'their bloody son'. It gave me a chance to say a rude word like 'bloody'. It felt really wicked.

That night a lone and probably the last bomber fleeing from a raid on London dropped a few small fire bombs onto the racecourse near Tattenham Corner. The flares from the bombs burning on the grass raceway could be seen from the bar. Ma Ash was infuriated. How dare Hitler drop bombs on her Epsom Downs. And she was equipped to do something about it. Leading her team of amateur fire fighters at the gallop and at full charge they left the pub to do their duty, cheered on by the more than slightly pissed contents of the bar.

Into the night they went with buckets clanging. Anyone who knew the location of the Derby Arms to that of Tattenham Corner knows it is quite a long way. Some hours later the brave team staggered into the bar exhausted and covered in mud, muttering that the bloody things had burnt out by the time they had got there. The pub filled with hilarious laughter. A few pints later everything was back to normal, apart from some hurt pride from the Langley Bottom fire wardens.

Mum and Dad became very friendly with Mrs Ash whose home 'Regma' was used by local racing lads who worked in the many racing stables nearby as lodgings, a real home from home for them, huge meals, everything homemade. Her tea table layout was fantastic—jam tarts, cream cakes, homemade jams, apple pies—you could hardly find room for your plate.

'Why don't you come and stay at our house at night instead of sleeping in those damp golf huts?' she asked, the ash from her cigarette hanging in a gravity-defying curve that would never fall even as she talked.

This must have seemed an excellent idea, as from then onwards we travelled the extra mile into Langley Bottom and the extra comfort of Regma, an attractive house with two bay windows, a nice porch with well tended gardens and a large orchard at the rear.

We were greeted by the large now grown-up family, sons—Snowy, amazingly white blond hair, age about thirty, his wife Polly, a painfully thin young woman but very kindhearted, daughter, Beatty, a lady my mother's age, but my size as she was of restricted growth, Doug, elder son rather deaf, her other sons away in the services. Her husband Reg was a quiet man and as Ma would not let him get a word in edgeways it was just as well.

I think it must have been the experience of the small fire bombs dropped on Tattenham Corner that made the Ash family feel that Hitler had singled them out for annihilation. For when we arrived that night they had arranged to all go to their Andersen Shelter for the night and suggested we should use their beds for ourselves. What a great idea, after suffering the blitz bombing in London their beds were about as safe a place you could find.

To see the Ash family in their shelter night after night with an old blanket over the small entrance, not huddled in fear, it was like a gambling den in there, table set out with candles and packs of cards, large brown quart bottles of brown ale stacked up in crates on the floor. Ashtrays everywhere full to overflowing, eyes squinting from the smoke as they gambled the night away. We slept in their beds for many weeks, and I don't remember a bomb ever being dropped on Epsom. We did eventually move back to the golf huts behind the Derby Arms Pub. I expect they became tired of sleeping in their shelter or ran out of money and beer.

The golf huts that we felt so safe sleeping in for all those weeks took a strange twist of fate.

Towards the end of the war, months after we no longer needed to leave London at night, the bombing had almost ceased. Hitler was losing fast, but his new terror weapon, the flying bomb, the V1 or, as we called it, the 'Doodle Bug', were being sent over as a last-minute hope of success. These pilotless aircraft were wonder-weapons from science fiction to us, no one ever believed a plane could fly so far without a pilot. Spitfire's could attack them with fire power, but one serious danger, the massive warhead in their nose could blow the Spitfire out of the sky the moment it exploded. One trick that pilots had devised was to fly alongside the V1, use their wing to tip the flying bomb over and out of control to explode hopefully on open countryside.

A situation like this occurred over Epsom Downs. A Spitfire in hot pursuit of a doodle bug, bravely flying alongside—which was very difficult and only achieved by the Spitfire diving at great speed onto the very fast target—tipped its wing over. The V1 going into an almost vertical dive straight for the Derby Arms, it ripped clean through the end of the building damaging some of the public bar where I sat on the piano singing 'Bless them all' and my rude word. The outside toilets were demolished as it continued to slide into our golf huts beyond, where it exploded turning them into matchwood.

The Derby Arms still stands today, very lucky that the fuse on the bomb was delayed enough to allow the explosion to occur after the initial impact. So were we as safe as we thought, sleeping so snugly in our golf huts for all that time. Little did we know their future. The saying at the time was that 'if a bomb has your name on, it will find you, no matter what you do'. Obviously our name was not on that one.

Epsom to me had become a perfect paradise so it was with delight that I learned mother had accepted Mrs Ash's offer for me to stay with her at Regma. The bombing had become extra heavy again so she felt it would be safer for me. My sister Jean, being only a baby, never left mother's side. It must have been a terrible stress for mother this bombardment every night nonstop. They had decided not to travel each night to Epsom but to stay in their shelter and take their chances like everyone else. Bombing had become a way of life by now, but for me to be safe and out of harm's way would have been important to her.

On arrival at Regma, my suitcase full with my clothes, my ration book in my hand ... here I go for another spell of evacuation ... but this time I wanted to go. I knew the area quite well by now, so felt at home straight away.

Mrs Ash showed me to my room. Well, not quite my room. I shared this room with three older men. In one corner was a large double bed, in this bed slept Tommy Reeves, a tall dark and handsome, black curly-haired, and very Irish jockey. How come he was tall you say? Because he was a steeplechase jockey. They are normal height and weight. My mother I think quite fancied Tommy. He was full of Irish charm and very handsome, was very attentive to her, quite a contrast to my Dad who showed her no love and had no idea how to flatter the ladies.

Tommy's room-mate was a stable lad named Hobo, called Hobo because of his unkempt scruffy appearance. They shared a large double brass bed (two men sharing the same bed in those days was not considered in the least bit strange). On the other side of the room was a single bed in which slept an older man whose name I have forgotten but his behaviour I have not. My bed, a single camp bed, was between the large and smaller beds in this by now very cramped room. I had not been there for more than a few nights before it happened. In the middle of the night I woke, and to my alarm could feel someone's hand in the bottom of my bed.

Now I knew nothing about homosexuals, but instinct told me to move as far away as possible. He never touched me apart from his hand sliding up my leg. I jumped out of bed, went over to Tommy's bed and woke him up.

'Can I come into your bed, please, Tommy,' I pleaded. He said nothing to this strange request, Just moved over, pushing poor Hobo nearer to the wall to make room for me.

Next morning I told Tommy and Mrs Ash what had happened. Tommy wanted to beat him up, Mrs Ash was going to call the police, but first they decided to confront him with the charge themselves. Naturally he denied everything, saying it was impossible to do what I said and that I must have been dreaming. My bed was next to his, the foot of my bed being alongside the foot of his bed, it would have been very easy for him to reach into the bottom of my bed, also I actually grabbed his hand and held on as he pulled away, so it was no dream. The only way he could reach into my bed was from the bottom. Too much of a coincidence.

As he was quite old and I was not the least bit upset—I just thought he was a dirty old man—he was told to leave Regma there and then. I think he felt he had got off lightly, as Tommy and Mrs Ash's sons would have beaten him up for sure if they'd been allowed their way. That was the custom in those days—instantly applied justice.

So it was not such a good start to my stay at Epsom. Mother was informed but no fuss was made. She knew the family there were wonderful people so no more was said.

Tommy Reeves became a bit of a hero to me from then onwards. He was so witty and with his film star looks was ready to fight anyone in the pub who showed disrespect to my mother. On one occasion, after a dance and quite a lot of Guinness, he wiped the floor with a fellow Irishman, who happened to make the near-fatal mistake of describing my mother's sexual appeal within his earshot, doing all this with his right arm in plaster to his elbow, having had a nasty fall from a racehorse the previous week.

It was Tommy's good looks that made me constantly aware that my fair and baby-fluff straight hair was never going to match up to Tommy's black thick wavy locks, so much like the Hollywood heroes I had seen in films. This vanity showed itself a few years later when I was about twelve years old. Tommy and our family were still good friends and after a weekend visit by Tommy and Snowy, I said, 'Oh, I wish I had wavy hair like Tommy's Mum.'

The next day I was sitting in the ladies' hair salon, my head covered with perm lotion, with about thirty electric wires connected to plugs that had my hair rolled around them. As I sat there with the plugs sizzling with the heat (they used electrically heated rollers then), my embarrassment was unbearable.

In my rush to look like Tommy my foolish mother had encouraged me to have a perm. I had no idea what was involved. I thought you just went there, a wave of the magic comb and you had wavy hair for life. I was shocked to hear it only lasted a few months. The ordeal over, I left the salon and walked home nearly in tears. The mass of tight curly frizz ball sitting high on my head looked nothing like

Tommy's sweeping waves. Friends of the family burst into laughter on meeting me.

'What have you done to his hair?' they would ask

But the worst was to come—school. I was ridiculed for weeks. Every day I would grease down the frizz as much as I could. It took weeks and weeks to fall out. Mother said it looked very nice. Well, she would, wouldn't she.

The village school in Langley Bottom was an all-corrugated tin building at the top of the hill. My first morning there was a bit uncomfortable for being the new kid involved being picked on by the Village kids—all from the pretty rough homes of the farm labourers. The answer was to trade with them. Coming from a dealer family I expect I had a natural ability to do a deal. All boys collected birds eggs. To amass a large collection was my ambition, so these kids could not afford to dislike me—as they were experts at bird nesting and I was a bigtime buyer up from London.

I was accepted into their gang and full membership allowed me access to the Camp. Opposite Regma was a large flint wall, on the other side a thick wood backing onto a golf course. It was in this wood we had the camp, the army used the adjoining land for war games training. This was an excellent source of unexploded thunder flash (imitation grenades), very much like large fireworks, many being left behind by the soldiers. Armed with these and bow and arrows, many battles were fought by us kids in these woods. Another regular place for our gang to meet was the large brick air raid shelter on the edge of the village. These shelters had no windows so it was pitch dark inside. A reinforced concrete roof and fitted out inside with bunk beds, three high on both sides—a perfect place for our gang to meet. In candlelight we would discuss the next daring escapade.

Epsom Downs in 1942 was open heathland combined with dense woodland, the racecourse running around and through this very attractive place. The grandstand no longer housed the Irish Guards. Instead there was now a new and much more interesting soldier stationed there. He chewed gum, wore a very smart uniform, always wanted to know if we boys had a sister, talked and looked as though he had just stepped straight from the silver screen we all worshipped every week at the cinema. He was a 'Yank'. We boys loved them and so it seemed did the girls. The saying at the time was 'Overpaid, oversexed and over here'.

If we spotted a Yank we would home in on them with, 'Hi, Yank—got any gum, chum.'

They were very friendly to us kids, always generous with their gum. I never ever remember not being given a few strips of gum from them. There was always the inevitable question, do you have any sisters, to which we always answered yes, two, eighteen and nineteen years old. This immediately gained their interest and possibly a few more sticks of gum. Which we chewed as we swaggered through the village, all talking with American accents out of the side of our mouths, mimicking the characters we saw in American gangster films.

Our gang would organise Yank-hunting raids. Yank hunting was quite fun as it combined two very important elements, the hunting instinct and sex. I did not quite understand about sex yet, but knew I would like to find out more about it. Our raiding parties would involve four or five boys. We would spread out in a line and move slowly across Epsom Downs. Sooner or later we would spot a Yank and his girl seeking out a quiet spot to lie in the sun.

Slowly the pack of hunters would close in on their quarry until we all had a front row seat to their cuddling. We would always be spotted before things became involved. A very angry Yank would look over his shoulder to see our smirking faces peering over the gorse bushes at them. We would all run like mad—and with an angry Yank soldier after you, you thought this is probably not a good time to ask him for gum.

Sex was never mentioned by my parents. You were expected to find out all you needed to know the best way you could. But the subject was so embarrassing to them they just left it out. Even at school we only talked about mice, never humans, so I had to find my own teacher. Well, the best teacher in our village was apparently a fourteen year old girl, Cathy Reedman. The older boys were constantly saying that they had, had 'it' with Cathy.

I kept thinking about 'it' and Cathy. I'm sure 'it' would be nice to do if I only knew how to do it. Cathy went to our school but being only nine years old myself, I had not mixed with her but as she was so popular with the boys, she was not surprised to find me walking beside her trying to appear much older than I was, on our way home one afternoon from school.

I don't suppose I blinded her with my charm at nine years old, but she did seem to like me enough to agree, as we passed a particularly grassy spot screened by thick gorse bushes, for us to sit down for a while. I started to kiss her and felt the excitement of what 'it' was obviously all about. As she lay back, her long dark hair spread attractively onto the emerald green grassy bank. Boy, this is 'it' I thought. Sliding my body onto hers I started to move slowly in a rhythmic way, she too by now was enjoying my attentions.

This is where I had a problem, I knew I liked what I was

doing but I did not know how to proceed to the next stage. This was big time for me—what else could be more exciting—so when Cathy said to me, breathing heavily, 'You can put it in if you want to,' I stupidly said, 'No I am quite alright as I am, thank you.'

I was too embarrassed to ask where and how. She jumped up very soon after that remark and stormed off, probably thinking these nine year olds are a waste of time. It was some years before Cathy would give me another chance on the grassy bank.

Village life in Langley Bottom evolved around the dusty hut. The dusty hut was the tin village hall, dancing there every Friday night a highlight for all to look forward to. The nickname dusty hut came about because of the dust that rose from the wooden floor as soon as couples started to dance. It became a haze that, combined with cigarette smoke, developed to a fog within minutes.

Here boy met girl in the age-old fashion way. It gave everyone an excuse to dress up in their best clothes, to see and be seen. Dressing up was quite a ritual for the Ash family.

Hours before the event suits would be taken off their hangers and pressed until you could cut your finger on the trouser seams. Blue pinstriped double-breasted suits would be brushed to look like new as you probably never had the coupons to replace them—with white shirts, a tiepin pinning the collar together under your tie to follow the latest fashion, black unbelievably polished shoes, looking like glass as the duster was strapped briskly over the toecaps for that final touch—the whole family were jostling for positions near the solitary mirror in the kitchen. Eager to apply as much dark green incredible strong-smelling Brillianteen to the hair as possible. In their tight jackets and very wide trousers, shoes shining like glass, the prime of Langley Bottom's manhood set off. To be covered in dust within minutes of arrival must have been very annoying.

On one occasion, just after the Ash boys had left for the big dance and, being impressed by their slick appearance, I opened their shaving cabinet. Unscrewing a jar of hair cream I slapped a mass of it on my hair, sliding the long black comb through my very fine hair until a large greasy quiff was standing up on top like a cockerel's comb. Meeting our gang later I felt quite grown up as we sipped brown ale from a large brown quart bottle of beer that one of the boys had managed to smuggle out that night.

'Let's go to the dusty hut.'

We all agreed, so half an hour later found us all looking through the window of the dusty hut with total fascination. The three-piece band was thumping away with the hit tunes of the time, 'In the mood', 'Three little fishes'—probably the silliest song ever written—all the Hollywood influence. We tried to relive the fantasy we saw on the screens every week, dancers would 'jitterbug', a frantic, almost acrobatic dance, with girls flying over their boyfriends' shoulders, stocking tops and knickers flashing to the delight of all the boys—although what appeared to be stockings would often be legs stained brown with an eyebrow pencil line up the back of their legs to simulate a seam. For, unless your boyfriend was a Yank, stockings were almost impossible to find. This was the exciting world of grown ups. I couldn't wait to join them.

It was a very warm evening, the window and door to the dusty hut were open wide to allow the dancers as much cool air as possible. By this time we boys had consumed the last of the bottle of beer which probably accounted for our boldness. Sneaking in the back door behind the band we settled down on the floor half hidden by the curtains. This was great, enjoying the music and going unnoticed until I started to feel sick. In a mad rush to get out I did not quite make it, throwing up just inside the rear entrance. Suddenly I was surrounded by angry dance officials.

The Ash boys were called over. 'He's drunk,' they were told. An exaggeration, I was just wobbly on my feet.

Ron Ash told me to go home. 'You will be in trouble when Ma hears of this.'

In bed that night I was terrified of the consequences. Next morning, to my delight, Ron said nothing at all about my mishap so I was off the hook. Only one other problem remained. I was unable to comb through my hair that morning, the hair cream I had slicked on my head so thickly the night before had not been hair cream but shaving cream. My hair had set hard, and my smart quiff lasted quite a few days.

It was about this time that I started to visit the racing stables of the once famous jockey, Johnnie Dines. He had a beautiful racing stables just outside Langley Bottom Village, high on the hill, perfect in every detail, the stables set in a 'U' shape with a large courtyard and adjoining paddocks.

Hobo and Tommy worked for him, Hobo as a stablehand, Tommy as his top jockey. Being invited to go with the boys was really something. it meant getting up very early on non-school days, 6am to get an early start, for there were two strings of horses to be cleaned, ridden out for exercise, properly galloped and timed by Mr Dines to see their potential for the next race meeting.

My job was to help. It was unpaid but very coveted by boys and I was very lucky to be allowed to go. Practical jokes were constantly being played on the younger members of his staff, new girls working there would often have their jodhpurs pulled down to their knees, stuffed head first down between bales of hay and left there screeching for help, until some kind soul who probably wanted a close up, came to their assistance.

One trick that could have proven fatal to me was when the horses were fed. These were racehorses, highly strung beautiful speed machines, not steady old plodders.

Given a bucket full of hot feed or a sack with dry chaff and corn, they would tell the new boy, feed No 26. Off I went, reached up, unslid the large bolt to the half door, stepped in to be faced by the bulging wild red eyes of the biggest black stallion in the yard. Once in I had to somehow get to his feeding trough—always at the furthest spot from the entrance door. He would nip at you, snort, charge, kick and if possible crush you against the stable wall to finish you off. He was lethal.

As I emerged bruised, bitten and battered, there were peals of laughter from the waiting stable lads who knew only too well what this horse would do. Looking back I could easily have been killed. I made sure I never fed that horse again.

Apart from the dangerous sense of humour, this was a wonderful place to work and I immediately decided I would like to become a jockey. To be a jockey you would have to spend five years as an apprentice, most boys living with ladies like Ma Ash as lodgers. It was a great life if you loved horses and were small. If you were normal in size you could only aspire to a jump jockey.

The problem with this side of the profession was you were always in danger of a nasty fall, no matter how good you were, it would happen. Tommy was a first-class jump jockey but had still broken about every bone in his body and was forever in plaster. As I was a nine to ten year old and some of the seventeen to eighteen year old boys were still only my size, my chances of being small and light enough to be able to follow a successful career in flat racing was pretty slim.

As I cannot say too often, living with Ma was just special. Her home was just full of happiness, there was always so much activity, full of bustle and laughter, the boys always joking with each other. At meal times these huge dinners would appear to be instantly consumed by starving stable lads.

Ma would flit in and out from the kitchen, her arms full of extra helpings to try to satisfy these hard-working appetites. She did all this usually with a twinkle in her eye and a three-quarter burnt-out cigarette, its ash still intact and defying gravity, refusing to fall. Probably the twinkle in her eye was induced by the cigarette smoke. As she talked, juggled hands, her cigarette moved about in rapid flicking movements, but never did the ash fall on to her starched white linen table cloth.

Card playing was a major pastime at Regma. Most nights her large dining table would be set up, cards shuffled, ashtrays everywhere, players tightly packed around the table, Ma very much in charge looking like a Las Vegas croupier. Within minutes the room was thick with blue smoke, yet nobody seemed to cough or feel the least bit distressed by the lack of air.

This was serious gambling, a week's wages could be lost in one night. My mum and dad would always join the players. Dad being quite addicted to gambling, it was during one of these late night card sessions that an incident occurred that could easily have ended my parents friendship with the Ash family forever.

Dad, excusing himself from the card table, made his way outside to the toilet. If my Dad went outside to a freezing cold toilet, it was something of a ritual, trilby hat on, overcoat with collar up, scarf wrapped tightly round his neck, leather gloves completed the picture. Outside a quick rush through the frosty air found him sitting down in the 'bog', his word for the toilet—stands for 'bottom of the garden', where most toilets would be found before indoor plumbing.

Now whether he had won or lost at the table we will never know, but while he sat there he started to count his cash. Dad always carried quite a lot of cash on him, it was some form of status to have a large roll of pound notes probably in excess of one hundred pounds. He would make a big show when buying a drink in a pub, revealing this huge bundle, peel off a pound, returning the rest into his inside pocket to the hidden gasps of all around. If a man carried as his spare cash an amount that would take them months to earn, he must be very rich indeed, so Dad felt a big shot (just like in the films again). I have known him to carry two or three one hundred pound bundles on him.

So this night in the toilet he was checking the bundles. Whether he had been drinking, or just careless I'm not sure, but horror of horrors, he left a bundle on the toilet floor. Returning to the smoke-filled room, it was not until some time later that he realised what he had done. Shooting up from the table, his face white with shock, he disappeared out the door at breakneck speed, only to return seconds later even whiter that before. But this time those angry eyes flashed at everyone in the room.

'Who's taken my money,' he screamed.

'What money,' was asked by a puzzled and taken-aback group of faces.

'The money I left on the floor of the bog. Sixty five pounds it was and one of you have taken it.'

It took all my mother's time to calm him down. If you wanted to break Dad's heart just separate him from one of his bundles. We never knew who took his money. Mother often said it probably fell from his pocket into the toilet pan and he flushed it away. She probably said that to make him feel even worse about it. Amazingly we still stayed friends with the Ash family and things carried on as usual, no more was mentioned about the unhappy event from that time on.

Dad always seemed to have the ability to make people dislike him, he lacked social charms but never lacked animal cunning that came with his upbringing in a wheeler-dealer world.

'Do it unto him before he does it unto you' was his watchword. He trusted no one and taught me by example to be the same. In a lot of ways he was right.

'A fool and his money are soon parted,' he would say. 'Never ever lend people money, don't trust anyone, don't believe what people brag about, they tell lies'. When young I thought he was too untrusting but now I know he was right most times.

In 1939 Dad bought a 1934 Morris Ten Four family saloon for the not immodest amount of £75. He used it throughout the war for small car hire work that did not need a large car, it was a pretty little car all shiny and black, but then all cars were black in those days. Dad's cars always looked immaculate. He spent hours and hours working on them until they shone and looked like new. It was not uncommon for Dad to use this car to visit Regma, and was admired by Tommy Reeves on many occasions. Rremember no one had cars then, Dad was the exception as he was allowed petrol coupons for his business.

Tommy really coveted this little car. He was allowed to sit at the wheel and imagine it was his, as one other of Dad's rules was nobody drives my car except me. Tommy's need for a car by now had reached a point of desperation. Being a successful jockey he could well afford to buy one, but then there was the problem, during the war factories were too preoccupied manufacturing Spitfires, so no cars were built between 1939 and the end of the war in 1945.

Dad's instinct for a tasty profitable deal was alerted immediately to Tommy's despair that he could not fulfil his heart's desire to own a car for the first time.

'I'll sell you the Morris if you like, Tommy,' Dad casually let drop in conversation. 'I could do with another bigger car now that we have so many weddings being booked in.' Soldiers on leave were rushing headlong into marriage which was great business for Parsons Car Hire Service.

'How much,' said Tommy.

'About three hundred and fifty,' said Dad, waiting for a thud as Tommy hit the floor.

To Dad's delight there was no thud and very quickly he was excitedly counting out £350 in pound notes on our kitchen table in Peckham. Can you imagine how much that was then? A few years earlier you could have bought a brand new semi-detached house in Blackfen, Sidcup for yes, you guessed, £350.

Now although Dad was reluctant to give anything away, most times when he sold a car he was very generous. Mum would always receive one large white £5 note, Jean and I would be given a ten shilling note each or, if this was a special deal, sometimes even a pound note. So sitting around the table waiting for our share of the loot was exciting. That magic moment was to be repeated many times when as a young man Dad taught me how to be a car dealer and I counted my share of the pound notes as well.

Tommy seemed very happy with his new if somewhat expensive new car for quite some time then, as so often happened, some discontent settled in. We arrived at Regma to see this now filthy dirty little car lying in the driveway, once Dad's pride and joy.

'Bloody thing won't start, will it!' exclaimed Tommy.

Dad checked it over and managed to start the engine. With an ungrateful grunt they all piled into this poor little motor car. There must have been six or seven squeezed into her until she was about to bust her springs. With a crashing of gears she started her long drive uphill to the Derby Arms, smoke pouring from her exhaust. In a few weeks they had wrecked this pretty little car.

That weekend an argument started between Dad and Tommy over the car. Tommy wanted his money back, a word that sent quivers down my Dad's spine. Tommy was big and my Dad was small but he looked mean with it. His eyes would flash and his fighting stance left you in no doubt he was ready to have a go.

Tommy was towering over Dad, very menacing, his dark Irish eyebrows squashed together in fury. 'Money back or I'll bash yer, I will.'

I was sure that for a second or two Dad thought shall I give him his cash back. But the very word cash back would have made Dad shudder at the awful thought. So into action he went his left arm shot out onto Tommy's shoulder with an almighty shove, sending him reeling back against the side wall of Regma.

Dad held him there for some time by the throat, his very strong hand nearly choking Tommy with his own tie, his right arm held back, fist clenched, ready to hammer into Tommy's face if any resistance was offered. Nothing was said. Tommy's face went white with fear as the blood drained from it. Tommy was quite a fighter. After quite a lot of beer, but cold sober, he was no match for Dad, his eyes flashing with unbelievable fury, had convinced Tommy to back down.

Ma, hearing the uproar and probably the thud as Tommy hit the wall, rushed from the house and in her usual courageous manner pushed herself between the two men. 'Don't be bloody fools, if you have to fight, do it outside my gate.'

The atmosphere was so difficult for all after this incident that Mum and Dad soon left Regma not to return for quite some time. Looking back as I am doing now, life seemed so simple then, yet Hitler was still bashing hell out of Britain. Obviously people still had their day-to-day problems like us all, but through childhood memories they all seemed such very happy people. Could it have been that they did enjoy the simple things, that at this very trying time the comradeship between people meant so much? We were fighting for our lives against the most terrifying tyrant the world had ever known. We really needed each other very much. Perhaps that's why it was so special.

Mrs Ash's husband Reg had died very suddenly. I was not really sad, I had never got to know him at all, he was a very quiet man completely dominated by his wife Sarah, but also quite happy in that situation. Very quickly a new man came into her life, or was he already there?

Charlie was his name, a short thin ex-jockey, now in the Royal Air Force, he embarrassingly quickly married her at the local register office and moved in to much resentment from her sons. During the next few months Charlie was thrown out and allowed back to Regma so many times we all lost count, he was eventually roughed up by her sons after some of Ma's money was missing, sent on his way and was never seen again.

I really cannot remember how long I spent living with Ma. I do remember how much I loved her, she was so kind and happy and had so much to do in her busy life but always found time for me. What was about to happen next was a sudden shock to me, so unexpected.

One day after returning home from school I unintentionally slipped into the house unseen by Ma and a lady friend talking in her parlour. They were deeply engrossed in conversation and just did not see me go up to my room.

On my return I heard my name mentioned. Standing quietly listening in the half light of the dark hallway, I heard Ma say, 'He's a little sod, and he's going home.'

What I had done to make Ma feel like this I really never found out, I suppose she was under quite a lot of stress with her second husband Charlie disappearing with her money. Perhaps I had been cheeky to her once too often, perhaps she just felt she could do without the work and responsibility of a young boy up to and into everything. I really wish I had not overheard their conversation because it really hurt me to hear her say she did not like me anymore. At the time I was convinced the reason I was to be sent home was because of a little mistake I had made one night a few days earlier.

What happened was this. In the middle of the night I awoke needing to relieve myself in a somewhat urgent manner. Under our beds there would always be a traditional chamber pot that was always in danger of being kicked over by a bleary-eyed boy on exiting from bed in the morning. Now let me make this clear from the start, on leaving my bed in the middle of the night, I felt I only needed a pee, which was fine as we would all pee in the pot if necessary. My problem was it did not end as a pee.

Oh, my God, I thought it's much more urgent that a pee. Spinning round I slammed my bottom on the small chipped enamel potty and nature took its course, perhaps I had eaten something that had disagreed with me. Well, to put it short, I had filled the pot to the brim. Not knowing what to do with it in the middle of the night, I carefully pushed it under the bed, well back to make sure I did not kick it over next morning. I really did intend to empty the pot next morning in the outside toilet which would have been some feat of balance I can assure you.

Well, I have the ability to forget most things. Seconds later, completely out of my head they go, I have never changed from then until now, I forget things very easily and I forgot the potty tucked well back under my bed.

How many days it lay there breeding bacteria I'm not sure but eventually the smell started to get noticed. And it did not need a bloodhound to find the spot. Ma managed it all on her own. Boy, was she mad. My explanation regarding my poor memory did not seem to have the calming effect that I hoped it would. To make matters worse she would not trust me to descend the dark staircase balancing the disgusting object. So poor old Ma had to make the perilous journey with its foul smell polluting her normally sweet-smelling home.

Do you think this may have been the turning point in Ma's decision to send me home? This was the second time having an accident involving a bowel movement had resulted in my being sent home. Aunt Daisy was not understanding either when my underpants contained a little more than passing wind had lead me to expect.

The Derby Arms in 1993. From these doors Ma Ash
challenged Hitler's might

Regma in 1993, now fitted with new porch and
up-market name misspelt Regmar House

A mock wedding photo. Left to Right: Dad, Mother, Friend, Ma Ash, Toney Ash and Uncle Jim. Dad and his brother in their Parson Car Hire Chauffeurs' uniforms

Left to Right: Toney Ash's wife, Connie Ash, Tommy Reeves, Mother, Showey Ash, Sister Jean and Beatrice Ash

CHAPTER TEN

BOYS OF THE BLITZ

I was sad to leave Regma and the excitement of our gang's adventures. Would I ever get a second chance to prove myself with Cathy Reedman, I thought as we drove home to Peckham through the bombed streets piled high with bricks and debris.

Once home I quickly adjusted to the routine. Bombers came over every night at dusk, continued bombing until dawn. Every night the same routine, out of bed as soon as the siren sounded, into the cellar, try and get back to sleep if you could. I would plead with mother to let me stay in bed. I never ever thought we would get bombed. We had been so lucky so far. Granddad Joe Parsons, also reluctant to go to his shelter during heavy raids, would just lie in his bed, turn over and say to hell with you, and happily go back to sleep—content with his philosophy that if a bomb hit him he would be asleep anyway.

Well, one night his philosophy came true. He was living in a terraced house in Camberwell at the time, sleeping on his own in his own bedroom when a very large bomb dropped, demolished the whole terrace in one mighty explosion. When Granddad woke, sitting boldly upright in bed, brushing the ceiling plaster, wooden laths, picture frames and about six inches of dust off his buried body, becoming suddenly aware that he was not yet in heaven, he decided to make a dash for the staircase that led down to the ground floor.

In the pitch dark he fumbled for the door handle. For a few seconds the reality did not dawn on him, as his hand went further and further into space.

'Gawd blimey,' he said. 'There's no bleeding wall there.'

Granddad's bedroom wall had been completely blown out. After the blast he had been left in his bed on the first floor. The air raid rescue teams were in hysterics at the sight of this old man in his nightshirt waiting patiently, sitting on his bed, high in the air, on a shelf, waiting for his rescuers to get him down. Even after this ordeal he still preferred his bed to a shelter.

London was now becoming a never-ending parade of rubble. Street after street, if not flattened, were so badly damaged that they were un-liveable. A terrible tragedy, but a bonus for us children, for this dangerous mangled mass of bricks and wood was absolutely perfect for adventure.

We would enter a bombed house through the smashed half-off-its-hinges front door, stepping over bricks and plaster everywhere, scamper up staircase after staircase, its banister railings completely missing, the stairs just hanging there, onto the roof where we would yell secret call signs to other members of our gang. Sometimes other gangs of kids would try to invade and destroy our special camps, very often underground, constructed from old doors, bricks, timbers covered with protruding nails ready to rip into our uncovered legs at any minute.

Inside would be a fireplace ideal for baking potatoes,

stewing tomatoes, cooking any tasty little something we could find at home. There would be a spot for candles and an old blanket would cover the entrance, inside we would share the odd Woodbine cigarette together passing it round and enjoying the feeling of being devilishly wicked. Dad's house was situated on the corner of Camden Avenue. The Avenue no longer exists, but was right opposite Lyndhurst Way, that to date is still there.

Camden Avenue led directly into East Surrey Grove. Here lived my best friend Jimmy Hughes. Jimmy, some nine months older than me, was a very popular boy, very clever at most things, he could always draw ships and aircraft extremely well, would construct the best push carts, (carts made from old boxes and pram wheels) that would career down hills with two boys on board at breakneck speed.

I always envied Jimmy's achievements and many times would knock on his door to ask if I could come in and help with some constructions or other going on in his father's wooden shed workshop. It might sound odd to say how important this workshop was to me—I would have killed to get in there, full of interesting tools all in their proper place, ready to transform some odd piece of wood into a usable enjoyable toy, model aircraft, ships, guns, scooters, pushcarts, all sorts of goodies came out of that shed.

Now Jimmy knew the power of attraction his Dad's shed had. He would often cruelly say no to my request to come in. I would look over his shoulder through to his garden to see there other boys all having fun. Fifty years later Jimmy and I are still good friends and I am in the process with Jimmy's help with the design, as he became a commercial artist when an adult, in constructing a weather vane depicting the Battle of Britain. This will be fitted to

Red Cow Farm when completed. I now have my own wooden shed with power tools, although not as neatly kept as Jimmy's. Just let him dare ask to come in, I have waited fifty years to see his face when I tell him no.

A new craze hit the streets of Peckham about this time, scooters, made from planks of wood and using ball bearing wheels, very small wheels, all steel, that would produce sparks when sliding to a halt in a deep skid, much to the envy of other children. Jimmy as usual was one of the first to construct such a scooter. Small groups of boys could be seen everywhere whizzing along the pavement riding prized scooters, each one highly decorated using flip-off bottle tops to spell out their names with a large 'number' in the centre. Scrap ball bearing wheels, scrap wood from the bomb sites, old bottle tops— produced this noisy speed machine. The noise was quite unbelievable when a small group of boys passed by, steel wheels clanging on every paving slab, sparks produced whenever there was the opportunity.

I pestered Dad for days to help me construct one of these scooters. I had the wood and the ball bearing wheels all ready, but as the days passed and still no help from Dad, my hopes of ever joining the other boys faded.

Then one day out of the blue Dad said, 'Freddie, your scooter's out in the garden.'

My heart leaped with joy. Rushing two steps at a time down the stairs into the garden unable to contain my excitement, there it was. The scooter, but not my dream machine. This scooter was made from thin red tin with white rubber wheels, had sissy-like white rubber hand grips that controlled girlish scroll-shaped handle bars.

Dad in his desperation to end my pestering had bought a scooter at the auction for a few shillings, splashed some red valspar paint over it, expecting me to prefer this to any scooter made from scrap. I don't expect for one minute that I hid my feelings of disappointment, but there it was. That's all I was going to get.

So down the steps and out onto the street it was pushed. Meeting up with the other boys oiling their wheels for the intended burn up around the block, I rolled up to them feeling like a little girl rolling so gracefully towards them using a gentle flowing skipping action, the white rubber tyres not making a sound as this wimpish machine whispered up to the boys.

Nothing was said to me but their looks told me all, as they sped off thundering down the pavement using short powerful thrusts with their legs. I followed on silently, my large rubber wheels gliding along like gossamer. I desperately wanted to belong, but as they disappeared into the distance, I turned the pretty red handle bars around and went home for tea.

Jimmy Hughes, my good friend, had an advantage over me at most times. His Dad was a wonderful example to him, able to teach him the correct way, perfection was very important to him in anything that they attempted. My Dad was the complete opposite. If there was a way to bodge it, that would be his way. When the fuses in our house made a habit of blowing, probably because Henry the Eighth did the initial installation, his answer was to jam large old type pennies into the fuses.

'That's stopped them blowing,' he would say, completely unaware that the house could burn down. As I said before, Dad was definitely born lucky.

Mother caught me one day face down, head over the bank of the East Surrey Canal trying to catch sticklebacks, little spiny fish that were abundant in the smelly water of this now unused Victorian canal. She whacked me, one whack for every yard, as she marched me home. I had been forbidden to go there as so many children had been drowned in its green stagnant water.

Mother realised that something had to be done about my fascination over these fish. Jimmy had by now constructed a lovely little fish pond in his garden using an old butler earthenware sink, removed from an old bombed house nearby. Using his imagination to form little rock pools and tunnels for the fish to swim through; the water sparkling clean, the fish bright red and healthy.

Dad decided to take me on a fishing trip to catch some sticklebacks and set me up with my own pond. We came back from the canal our bucket overflowing with fish.

'How can we make a pond Dad?' enquired a thrilled-to-bits little boy.

'Easy son,' said Dad. Into his garage he disappeared, returning almost immediately with a large 5 gallon oil drum. As we filled the drum I could see the large blue bubbles as oil rings floated to the top. Being careful not to cut my hands on the jagged edges of the drum where Dad had hacked out the top, I carefully lowered my fish into the oily water.

'They'll be alright,' said Dad. 'Used to mucky water they are.'

Looking at these fish swimming against the oil slick, fresh oil bubbles bursting all around as they gasped for breath, I remembered Jimmy's crystal clear, delightful little pond. Ssomehow my one was not the same with its Esso oil in large white letters on the side. Next morning all the fish were floating belly up on the now congealed surface, dead as dodos.

Jimmy and I seemed to have the ability to find ourselves

in endless situations that without intention would get us into trouble. Mum and Dad one afternoon looked at Jimmy and me playing in my garden using our tin bath, full with water and our imagination to relive a sea battle scene we had recently seen at the cinema.

'We are going out for a couple of hours,' she said. 'Don't get up to anything you two.'

'No, Mum,' said I, meaning it this time. Now I would very much like to blame Jimmy for what was about to happen but in fairness, we were both keen to make the battle seem more realistic.

'Let's make bows and arrows and shoot at the tin toy ships floating in the bath.'

In no time at all we had cut boughs from a nearby tree, shaped arrows and, with string from mother's cupboard, strung our bows. Now the action was much more fun, firing the arrows at each other's ships this seemed just like a real battle at sea.

It was then we made out fatal mistake.

'Let's tie meat skewers to our arrows and really sink them!'

Minutes later steel spiked arrows were being fired from full stretched bows at toy ships floating in mother's galvanised bath. For each time we managed a direct hit, three would miss their target altogether.

It was some time before we realised that the ocean was dropping rather rapidly around our sea battle. Minutes later our ships were resting on the bottom of the tin bath and into view came the cause—the whole bottom of the bath was peppered with tiny holes from the near misses from our arrows. Desperate to know what to do, we hung the bath back up on the wall and said nothing. Mother was livid when she found out next bath night. All was well in the end as Granddad George repaired the bath by soldering the holes water tight again.

This is just an example of how things go wrong for you as a child. On another occasion, Jimmy and I spent the whole afternoon digging a hole in my garden. We were down to our chins in this hole when Mum and Dad returned.

'It's our camp, Mum, we only need the roof to finish it off.'

'Fill the bloody thing in,' Dad demanded.

Parents are so unreasonable aren't they?

CHAPTER ELEVEN

CAMBERWELL BEAUTY

'Titserlina, Titserlina', the memory of her blouse buttons bursting, full breasted figure still remains strongly in my memory.

She had blonde hair, was quite tall, well covered to plumpish figure, probably not much older that I was at the time, but amazingly well developed for her age. Her real name I was never to know, for to us boys she was always 'Titserlina' because of her huge breasts. They hung in her blouse like ripe grapefruits that swung and bounced in an hypnotic way when she ran.

All the boys at school were fascinated by her, she would be followed everywhere. Titserlina had a very mousy little friend, all skin and bone a complete contrast to our lovely voluptuous dream girl. They both lived in Lyndhurst Way opposite my home and I would see her pass by everyday and yearn for her. God, how I wanted to investigate those hidden delights, I was not unusual, every boy in school felt the same way.

Titserlina just loved all the attention she received, holding her voluptuous charms hard out in front of her as she walked past us pop-eyed boys at school every day. She would never be short of escorts to walk her home after school. The older boys seemed to be more in favour than I was, but undeterred I would always make a point of being as near as possible to her on my way home from school. All the boys fancied her like mad, it would be very unusual to find her alone, her friend was often alone but who cared anyway.

To my amazement and delight one afternoon after school there she was with her skinny friend walking quietly down the road not a follower in sight. My friend and I casually drifted in their direction, our excitement grew and grew until we came face to face with them.

I had spoken to her in the past but no more than a stupid passing remark, this time I would really not miss my opportunity. She seemed to really like me and became quite flirty, joke's and cheeky remarks were exchanged, somehow I managed to manoeuvre the conversation onto doing 'IT'.

This produced lots of giggles from the girls, us boys became quite excited, we were convinced we were on a winner at last.

'Well, what about you and me doing "IT",' said I to Titserlina, my knees starting to tremble at the thought.

To my delight she said, 'yes, she would love to, but …'

'But what,' said I.

More giggles from the girls. 'You wait there,' they said. They moved a few yards to our left. 'We will write the reason on the pavement for you to see.'

Mystified we waited until, using chalk, the message was written. As we approached they ran into the distance giggling loudly. On the pavement were the two large letters 'MP'.

As we boys walked away I said mystified, what had the Military Police got to do with it anyway. Perhaps we were not quite ready for such things yet.

I had now at last left Oliver Goldsmith School and was attending Sumner Road School for Boys. I hated both schools equally so nothing had changed, I do believe that the only time they moved me up a class was because I began to look ridiculous, towering above the smaller kids. We can't leave him here for ever they must have thought so let's put him up a class.

My short-term bad memory always held me back so when I left school at fourteen years of age, it was the best thing for me. For this boy, life would teach me far more than school ever could.

In the meantime, at school I had one other serious problem, a thug called Charlie Secker, a big tall kid with huge fat thighs that filled his short trousers to splitting point. My skinny thighs hanging down wrapped in underpants that insisted on falling down below my short trousers no matter how many times I pulled them up, combined with a body mother always said was pleasantly slim, yet everyone at school called me 'Tin Ribs'.

I was no match for Charlie. He bullied me with great delight at every opportunity he got, to the extent that I disappeared as soon as he came into sight I was really scared of him and he knew it.

Despite my efforts to keep out of his way he tracked me down in the playground and in front of all the school said he was going to beat me up after classes that afternoon.

Petrified I tried to slip out unnoticed only to find Charlie Secker and a mob of boys blocking my way home in the small alleyway near the school. Pushed into the middle of a crowd of jeering boys confronted by the awesome Charlie, fists raised, knuckles white and frighteningly large pushed into my face.

My thoughts were—how can I talk my way out of this, to fight meant a beating for sure. Before I knew what was happening I was pushed from behind with great force by bodies unknown, anxious to get the fight underway. My fist at the time was pointing in the general direction of Charlie's nose. The mighty push from behind sent my knuckles slamming into my opponent's face, blood spurted from his nose, he staggered back with total amazement and disbelief on his face and at that very moment our teacher appeared at the far end of this alleyway, the crowd dispersed within seconds.

The next day arriving at school, expecting Charlie to be waiting for me ready to finish me off, I slid into class hoping to go unnoticed. To my amazement I was considered a hero, all the boys in school were saying I had beaten up Charlie Secker. He completely ignored me from then on.

School to me was about the most boring thing in the world. Everyday as I walked to school, my gas mask in its little cardboard box over my shoulder, I would be dreaming of other exciting things to do in life. In class I would stare out of the window hoping the green fog haze would become so bad we would be sent home. Fogs owing to the coal fires in London were so bad at times the sky would become green.

'Stop daydreaming Parsons,' Mr Wilfred our teacher would demand.

Little did he know that my daydreaming would motivate me later in life, to follow through on those dreams, to have tenacity to stick with those dreams, that those daydreams are the spark of life, that if you can dream it, you can do it, but he wanted me to forget those dreams, I'm so glad that I did not.

One lunchtime, after probably spending the morning at school daydreaming, I started the short walk home, school dinners were tasteless and boring with dishes like macaroni cheese—yuck—going home for lunch was much nicer.

About half way home on a clear blue cloudless day, the streets busy with people going about their day to day business, stepping around piles of debris and broken glass from the previous night bombing, trams rattling by. The brave and determined Londoner safe after his night's ordeal but this day we were not as safe as we thought.

No air raid warning had been sounded, but as I heard the deep throbbing roar of a low-flying aircraft in the distance a sense of fear crept over me. Luckily for me I was very close to the entrance of a street air raid shelter with its large white 'S' painted on a black background high on its wall. Before I had my chance to take cover it was onto us. Flying at tree top level I saw the black cross insignia of a Fokker Wolf 190 German fighter plane, its guns now firing in spasmodic bursts roar overhead.

Within seconds it was gone, heading towards Catford, where it dropped a 500lb bomb on a school killing many children. In fairness to the pilot a factory and a school from the air must look very much alike but at the time this was just what we would expect from a cruel enemy. I arrived home much to Mum's relief. That was as close as I was to get to Hitler's No 1 fighter plane. With no air raid warnings given I can only imagine he slipped in low under our radar cover. Apparently this type of incident was not uncommon.

Dad's taxi business was thriving, although driving around London during the war was full of hazards. On one occasion leaving Paddington Station a bomb dropped so close, that his car virtually left the ground as he was blown across the road. He said at the time there was a big bang and his steering on the car suddenly became unbelievably light. Seconds later he was on the opposite side of the road. On many occasions he would collect American Servicemen from these London stations and take them to their destinations and often as a tip they would kindly give him food knowing how short we were, this was gratefully accepted.

Returning home one night, a large round quite tall tin was placed on our barley-twist kitchen table.

'What's in it,' we all enquired.

'Sausages,' said Dad, 'a present from a Yank.'

The tin opener was quickly in use and sure enough inside were these unusual very long sausages in a thick jelly, heated and consumed that evening they were delicious. We had never seen sausages like these before. I did not know at the time but I had just eaten my first frankfurter.

Life in our house at night evolved around the wireless. Each night the news would be listened to with stern silent faces children forbidden to make any noise as details of the war unfolded. How many planes we had lost over Germany in the now colossal night raids, inflicting terrible retribution on Nazi Germany for the misery we had been suffering for so long. News out of the way, light entertainment would be listened to. Shows such as, Henry Hall's Guest Night, Saturday Night at 8 o'clock, ITMA, a comedy show with many catch phrases, used every day that helped keep our spirits up during those dark times—my favourite was 'Into Battle', true stories about war.

Now do not feel sorry for us because we were without television, remember on the wireless the scenery is so much better, the mind transported us anywhere we wanted to go. A comedy show with a more sinister side to it was Lord Haw Haw, transmitted late at night from Nazi Germany,

Lord Haw Haw was an Englishman and a traitor living in Germany, he transmitted his programme full of propaganda intended on demoralising the British and weaken our resolve to fight. His real name was William Joyce. He was brilliantly nicknamed Lord Haw Haw mainly because of his monotone droning voice. Always introducing his radio programme with 'Germany calling—Germany calling', no one took him seriously, but he was compulsive listening.

Dad always liked to tune into hear his babblings. 'Wonder what old Haw Haw has to say tonight,' twiddling the knobs on the radio until the squeaks and whines stopped.

Suddenly clear as a bell came 'Germany calling—Germany calling.'

We all settled down to listen to his latest reports on the war, always the usual thing was said.

'Why are we resisting the might of Germany, our situation is hopeless they really want to be our friends.'

No one believed him, but he did have a fascination, if only to hear what he would come up with next. In the past he had often predicted events that were to happen in the war with alarming accuracy. One night when he mentioned the Camberwell beauty, we all sat bolt upright in our chairs as he droned in his dull depressing voice.

'The Camberwell beauty will cease to exist.'

We all knew the Camberwell beauty he was referring to. It was the logo of Samuel Jones Factory, no more than a quarter of a mile from our home, at this time in full swing manufacturing war materials. On its wall in a huge mosaic was a butterfly called a Camberwell beauty.

That night the expected air raid started quite late, we were all in our cellar shelter in readiness for Haw Haw's prediction and we were soon not to be disappointed. The wailing siren screamed its high then low pitched screech for quite some time before the guns opened up. Thud, thud into the pitch black night sky they thundered omitting flash after flash, lighting up the clouds as they sprayed the sky with jagged steel splinters hoping to pierce the air frame or destroy the engines of these unseen deliveries of death on their nightly visit to our City.

Dad and I would often stand in our front doorway at the top of the stairs to our cellar and watch the raid in total fascination. Chunks of shrapnel would strike the pavement omitting showers of sparks, aircraft would be illuminated by criss-crossed search lights as they dived to avoid the anti-aircraft batteries, desperately trying to get their range. If bombs started to fall too close, we would tear down the stairs and take cover but otherwise we would stay and enjoy the excitement.

As soon as the all-clear siren had been sounded I would dash outside with a torch to try to locate the shrapnel lying on the street. Boys had large collections of these pieces of jagged steel that would be exchanged at school the next day. A real prize would be a complete shell nose cap in solid brass these would only be found in soft earth that enabled them to stay intact after falling 20,000 ft. But this night we were to be the centre of destruction, the bombs started to fall in sticks, you heard the scream as each bomb fell followed by a mighty explosion.

One, far away, two, much closer, three, God that one was close, then our breath held for number four. Would this one get us or not. Seconds later the explosion, it had passed over us this time. Everyone breathes again until ten minutes later the whole procedure starts again, that night never seemed to end, but as dawn cracked through the raiders left.

Dad and I wrapped our scarfs round our necks and stepped out into the dawn light. Total devastation everywhere, whole streets behind our house had disappeared, a huge crater had appeared opposite Jimmy Hughes house, half of the houses on his street had completely disappeared. It was almost impossible to walk down the centre of the roads because of so much debris. Streets were cordoned off with white tapes with unexploded bomb signs everywhere.

'There's a whole family trapped in the cellar of that house,' said Mr Beckett, his special police uniform covered in white plaster dust. 'there is gas and water escaping, and we are worried about getting then out before the cellar fills with water or there is an explosion.'

Sadly some people died because of this before being rescued.

Making our way the best we could into Southampton Way, the picture was repeated, smoking ruins everywhere, ambulances bumped their way along the rubble strewn streets trying to reach the air raid wardens in their dark blue boiler suits, their heads and shoulders deep into brick rubble holding the hand of some poor person waiting to be dug out by eager helpers, quiet, a shout would go out, silence, total silence would fall over the previously noisy scene.

A faint cry would be heard from deep below the rubble.

'OK, love, don't worry, we will soon have you out,' came the reassuring voice from the wardens above. More frantic digging.

As we walked the streets that hazy morning I remember how we hated the Germans for what they had done to us. It was almost light by now, the early morning sun falling against the thick smoke drifting across the sky from so many fires.

'I don't believe it,' said Dad 'She's still there.'

As the smoke cleared, this beautiful butterfly stared at us high on the wall of Samuel Jones Factory.

They never got the Camberwell beauty after all, they never got her. We felt we had won a great victory despite Haw Haw's prediction. Despite all we had endured he had not destroyed the Camberwell beauty. The factory was hardly damaged, Peckham was cleared up in a few weeks, we were more determined than ever to beat the enemy.

Lord Haw Haw was tried and convicted after this war as a traitor—we hung him—much to the delight of the population. Years later the Camberwell beauty was removed from the factory wall before demolition and later re-sited in a place of honour in the Borough of Camberwell for all to see.

CHAPTER TWELVE

―――――――

CHRISTMAS WITH MY BARMY AUNTS

In the midst of all this bombing life had the amazing ability to carry on very much as usual, mother would be busy working with her sewing machine to 'make do and mend' the catchphrase to encourage the population to repair and restyle their clothes.

'Dig for Victory' was another.

Granddad George had his vegetable allotment, which meant we always had fresh vegetables.

Yet another was 'Careless talk costs lives' to encourage the population to be aware there were a lot of spies about.

Well, careless talk nearly cost Mr Wilday his life.

Johnny Wilday, one of my friends living quite close to my home was his youngest son. Johnny a frail boy about my age, his poor bent body crippled with spinal tuberculosis, although young boys are notoriously callous, our group always felt sorry for Johnny. We all without exception treated him very kindly and included him in all our games. The fact that he always had more toys than us, plus a powerful air rifle, also helped to oil the wheels of our kindness.

Johnny's dad ran a small cycle repair shop in East Surrey Grove quite close to Jimmy Hughes home, so this little shop was in the centre of all our boyish activities. Opposite was the large bomb site we used as our playground and the location of many of the camps we boys used for our get-togethers.

Now getting back to 'Careless Talk Costs Lives', some careless talk had been said about Mr Wilday and the very voluptuous lady who lived on the corner of East Surrey Grove. Her house the end of terrace was next to the corner shop, Comptons the Newsagent. Mr Wilday on passing her house was no doubt drawn by her more-than-ample bosoms, into a little more than just conversation with the lady. Spies come in many forms and most of the spies in this street wore large wrap around aprons, always their hair in curlers and wore big woolly slippers, not much went unnoticed by them, they spent their whole day peering around their net curtains.

It was not long before Mr Wilday's visit were logged by these suburban 'Super Spies'. Mrs Wilday informed of her husband's philandering, went into battle like a 'bat out of hell'. This all happened one afternoon as we boys returning for our tea passed the battle scene.

Mrs Wilday, after pounding on her rival's door with her large fists (she also was a big lady), 'Come out, you dirty bastard,' she bellowed.

More hammering on the door, until a white-faced Mr Wilday shot out. Not a word more was said to him as he made a hasty retreat back to his home opposite. By this time a large crowd had formed in the street outside her house thoroughly enjoying the spectacle, especially the spy cell of hair netted, aproned, old biddies hoping for blood.

'Come out you cow,' bellowed Mrs Wilday, by this time

throwing anything she could find in the small front garden at the house and windows.

Eventually an upstairs window opened, through which the head and shoulders and ample bosoms of a woman appeared.

Mrs Wilday challenged her with all her evidence. 'Have you or haven't you?' she bellowed.

'Yes,' said the woman. 'He's done me many a time and I loved it' ... said as arrogantly as she could with a tormenting smirk on her face.

Mrs Wilday was like a bull looking for a matador, she charged up and down pounding on the door calling her all the names she could think of, but her tormentor had no intention of coming outside to face such anger, in the end she stormed off calling out 'Whore, whore'.

By this time I would expect Mr Wilday had locked himself in his garden shed seriously considering suicide as an alternative to facing his wife's return. I feel that if Mrs Wilday's anger could have been directed against Hitler the war would have been over a lot sooner.

Christmas during the war was extra special for us all, a time to really indulge ourselves using all the spare food we had hoarded for a real spread at Christmas. We even kept our own chickens, feeding them on scraps and potato peelings for months before to fatten them up for our big feast. The only problem was that on Christmas day no one wanted to eat them. We all felt sick to see our two chickens that for months we had called them by their pet names, all brown and sizzling on the large plate in the middle of the table.

Christmas night was very exciting for us, many members of the family would arrive for our Christmas party. Mother's two sisters Ann and Jessie, Nan and Granddad

George, my cousins Johnny and Jessie, My Uncle Stan, neighbours and other friends and relatives would make up the party.

We always had an Christmas tree that reached the ceiling. Most important that, it's not the same unless it was this tall. Granddad George would dress up as Father Christmas using my mother's red dressing gown, black wellington boots, with a cardboard mask attached to a red crêpe paper hood. I remember being terrified at Granddad's twinkling eyes as they moved about behind the mask, but we never questioned, quite happy to accept the gifts, enjoying the magic that only children can feel at Christmas. My grandmother, a gentle and dear lady, had a stepsister called Auntie Flo. Auntie Flo was the black sheep of the family and I think looking back was quite a bit barmy.

She would say to me, 'I'm your Auntie Flo from Brazil where the nuts come from.'

See what I mean.

She was a thin bony woman, very noisy with a crackling witchlike voice, always smelt of snuff which would be caked around her nose in brown lumps. Down the front of her clothes would be snuff powder that had fallen there from the frequent occasions she had sprinkled snuff onto the back of her hand prior to taking a gigantic snort propelling the powder into her nasal passage under great suction. On her face she had a number of large wartlike moles with black curly hair growing from the centres and she always, much to my revulsion wanted to smother me with kisses.

'Oh, come here, you lovely boy,' she would say. 'Give your aunt a big kiss.'

Being pulled into that snuff smelling body and feeling those hairs rubbing against my cheek, combined with a disgustingly wet kiss implanted with rattling false teeth was difficult to endure.

'Oh, he's shy,' said Aunt Flo, as I pulled away at the earliest chance I had to escape.

Now Auntie Flo had a checkered background, it was said in the family that she had been a prostitute when young in the early 1900s. I can just imagine her with a bustle, tiny bonnet hat, swinging her parasol down the strand, 'want a good time darling', the warts would have been beauty spots then, her wet kisses no doubt very much in demand, snuff being commonly used by so many people at the time would have made her odour go unnoticed.

'I'll give you a good time for half a crown, I will, love.'

To be crushed into her bodice in those days would have been good value at half a crown, apparently she was very successful with plenty of money and nice clothes, but was a constant embarrassment to her family, respectability being very important in those days.

Auntie Flo had all the vices and thoroughly enjoyed them all I'm sure, one of her favourites, drink. She could drink like a fish, her preferred poison being gin. She was alive in the days when you could 'be drunk for a penny' 'dead drunk for two pence'. This was the advertising slogan outside the old gin palaces, much in favour in Victorian times, where gin gained its name as mother's ruin. The gin palaces would provide entertainment, drink and a bawdy time for all and was possibly where Auntie Flo learned her trade.

Auntie Flo's husband, a short thickset man, was a burglar by trade. As a boy, and being told that he was a burglar, I imagined him climbing over rooftops at night dressed in a black and yellow striped pullover, a small black face mask with a bag over his shoulder marked swag, that's how they always looked like in my Beano comic. He must have been quite a high class burglar because in later life Auntie Flo had some very valuable antique furniture that they had not realised was of any value at the time.

They both enjoyed drinking and frequented the local pubs staggering out at closing time singing their way home. My Dad told me that often women on leaving pubs, bladder's full and inhibitions low, would squat in the gutters lift their long skirts up around their waist and urinate. There was no need to lower their underwear because the fashion at the time was crutchless drawers, literally two separate legs held together by a single string around their waist. The fashion must have been doubly useful to Aunt Flo at times.

To be fair to Auntie and Uncle, they were always very jolly people. I suppose regular visits to the pub helped to jolly then along most times, but sometimes the drink would make her aggressive, as it did one Christmas. Mother deciding to have Christmas at our home that year, decided to invite Auntie Flo, probably with some intrepidation as to the outcome. The Christmas party was in full swing, we children having been sent to bed, which was no disappointment to us, as we all jumped into a double bed in mother's bedroom, with no intention of sleeping. Lots of bouncing on the bed and pillow fights followed, completely out of sight of grown ups.

It was then that we heard raised angry voices coming from the rooms below.

'Shut up, you old bag,' and 'Cow, cow, you bloody old Tom cat, get her out the door.'

Rushing to the front windows, we kids looked down at the scene below. There was Auntie Flo being held by her collar and the back of her dress by Granddad George, one mighty heave and down the fifteen front steps she went landing in a heap at the bottom. Uncle followed.

'I'm sorry, Bill,' he said to Granddad. 'You know what she's like when on the gin.'

The last I saw of Aunt Flo that Christmas was a very angry, staggering lady shouting abuse back at us, flicking her fox fur stole over her shoulder. She disappeared in the direction of Camberwell with Uncle following on trying to calm her down. We children were never to know the cause of the eviction of Aunt Flo, but it was some time before the event was forgotten.

Amazingly colourful characters were friends of my parents during these years. Not the least were a lady and gentleman called Lil Pilchard and Blind Fred. Now I ask you, where do you hear names like that today. Lil Pilchard was probably the ugliest woman ever born, she had a face that would have frightened the daylights out of Dracula himself. Very thickset, her head and neck being as if one, she always wore the same 1920's no-shape straight dress with a sash on the hips, a coat would match, low healed shoes and a typical 1920's po hat pulled down over her ears completed the outfit.

Compared to Lil Pilchard Auntie Flo was a raving beauty. The warts with hair were bigger and more curly, her very full rubbery lips were always wetter, she too insisted on crushing me into her ample bosoms. There was an absence of smell of snuff from her, but this was a disadvantage as it allowed a strong odour of last weeks knickers to invade my nostrils instead.

'Give us a kiss, you lovely boy…'

Same struggles from me.

'Hasn't he grown? Soon be bigger than his dad he will,' she said.

Boy that remark gets boring I thought.

Her husband Blind Fred—he was always referred to as Blind Fred, never just Fred—blind since birth. It was said at the time that he could have had an operation to restore his sight in the past, but she would not hear of it, in case he saw her ugliness he would no longer have loved her and love her he really did.

A very kind happy man, always so gentle to this very ugly unfeminine woman. It's so sad to think his love could have changed with his sight restored. Or would it have? I would like to think not as they were so happy together. Blind Fred earned his living by piano tuning. He would visit our house on regular occasions to tune our upright piano. Mother had taught herself to play as a girl. She could play most of the tunes of the day without music quite well, except for the all-too-often wrong note that gave the song a very comical appeal.

One story that has always appealed to me was about Lil Pilchard and Blind Fred's wedding day. Mother and father attended the wedding and also the reception afterwards. This was held at their home using the front room for the party. The front room was every wife's showpiece, always kept in perfect condition, highly polished rexin three-piece suite (rexin a forerunner to plastic, was the poor man's leather0, barley-twist tables, highly polished brass or copper, gave the room an inviting glow.

But it was not for use—only on very special occasions—then your special guest would be ushered in, to be suitably impressed with the owners' opulence. The wedding party for Lil and Fred was a great success. No doubt Lil was not thrilled to bits to gain the family name of Pilchard, although I should think it was quite a rare name. Not many Pilchards about are there?

Late into the night the party goers enjoyed themselves, much drink was consumed the tables by now full to overflowing with large brown quart beer bottles, their stone screw stoppers discarded. In the corner of the room would have been the wooden crates ready to stack the empty bottles in for their return to the off licence the next day. There was to be no honeymoon holiday for Lil and Fred. It was difficult enough to provide a home, there would be no extras to pay for an unnecessary honeymoon.

They were quite happy to spend their first night of marriage upstairs in their own bedroom. As the revellers were making no attempt to leave, unable to control their anticipation any longer, they excused themselves from their guests. No sooner had the loving couple's footsteps reached the landing above, the party below became unusually quiet. Smirking smiles were exchanged between my dad and other friends sitting around the room.

It was not long before the sounds they were all waiting for started. Ding dong, ding dong came the rhythm from the bells the rotters had attached to the spring of their large brass bedstead. Ding dong, ding dong. When Lil dived under the bed to remove the bells she was to find their brand new china chamber pot had been filled to the brim with shandy. Floating in the pale yellow liquid were walnuts and toilet paper.

To finish off their evening of bad taste, alarm clocks had been hidden in drawers, all set to go off at different hours during the wedding night. Poor Lil Pilchard. I was never told if she was seriously angry or took it all in good fun. The party goers below continued their revelling until dawn, content in their thoughts that they had sent Blind Fred off in style.

Life for me was looking up, I had acquired a bicycle

secondhand for 30/-. This meant that to visit Grandmother I could ride there instead of the long tram journey. It was quite hard work riding from Peckham, over One Tree Hill to Nan's house, No 24 Lessing Street, Crofton Park. Many happy hours were spent there with my Aunt Nance who lived in the top half of the house, with my Aunt Jess who lived opposite in a similar type of house. All very cosy—my two cousins Jessie, two years younger than I and my young cousin Johnny, six years younger, were fun to play with.

Grandmother's kitchen was wonderfully cosy, there was a large cast-iron cooking range always highly polished with black lead, a metal polish that shone brightly when burnished with a dry cloth afterwards. The hearth would be whitened with hearth stone, creating a contrast. She could cook and boil kettles, the open fire hole was wonderful for toasting bread at breakfast time. An ever ready oven, complete with constant hot water, the range would burn anything, so was a good waste disposal as well.

Christmas was a special time at Nan's, her large front room made a prefect party room, all the family would gather, pockets bulging with their Christmas club money recently paid out by Granddad George. This Christmas Club was only a family club, we paid Granddad a modest amount every week which he held in a tin box hidden in a cupboard under the stairs. Come Christmas we divided out the cash according to how much each individual had paid in over the year. Mum would receive around £15. I remember my share was about £1.25p. This meant that Christmas would be a lot jollier than without it.

Well, one Christmas we really thought we were without it. When Granddad went to his 'hidey hole' the tin was gone. He could not believe his eyes. The family were called together, we sat around the room looking very glum.

Granddad opened the discussion with very few words. 'I'm giving whoever took the money until tomorrow morning to put it back. If it is not there I will call the police in.'

All eyes moved to Aunt Nance. How could it be anyone else, she was the only one in the house, there had been no break-in, we knew it was her. I loved her very much, she was a super aunt but she just could not resist temptation where money was concerned. Dad had found money missing from his till when as a young girl she had worked in his pet shop in Brixton. Nan some months earlier had trusted Aunt Nance to pay the rent on her house as she was working herself at the time. Aunt Nance had forged the entries in the rent book and pocketed the money. They were many months in arrears before Grandmother found her out.

Aunt had such a friendly way with her that she was quickly forgiven, amazingly. Nan even forgave her when her engagement ring disappeared. Aunt Nance helped her to search the whole house, all the time knowing that a few days earlier she had taken the ring to the local pawn shop and had received money for it. It was some months later that Grandmother saw her engagement ring in the pawn shop window. She had to buy her own ring back yet still Aunt Nance was forgiven.

So this time we all knew who to point the finger at.

'If the money is returned by tomorrow morning, no more will be said,' repeated Grandfather, everyone nodding in agreement.

We all wanted our Christmas money, no one wanted to see Aunt Nance arrested for theft, we all loved her too much for that. If ever you needed a sympathetic ear she would be there for you. She was a warm friendly caring female version of the lovable rogue and we did not wish her harm, but it would be nice to get our money back as well. Looking back she must have had a problem, she stole first and thought later.

The following morning sure enough on the kitchen table Granddad found the cash box. He opened the tin to find almost all of the money still there. A small amount was missing, probably just enough to clear Aunt's debts, we were all very relieved to receive most of our money. Christmas went on as if nothing had happened, blood is thicker than water I suppose.

When I think of Aunt Nance dancing with the family that Christmas, she must have been able to completely forget the anguish she gave us all a few days earlier.

Children of the war, 1944. Left to Right: Freddie, Cousin Jessie, Cousin Johnny, Sister Jean and Gyp the dog.

CHAPTER THIRTEEN

DODGING DOODLE BUGS

Life for me still evolved around Jimmy Hughes, our camps, everyday a new adventure. One fun thing for Jimmy and I was to climb to the top floor of a recently bombed house. This was pretty dangerous on its own. We would find the largest object we could and gradually move into the window, then heave-ho, out it went. The destructive delight on our faces as it disintegrated on the concrete below would have brought more than a frown from a policeman if caught. In those days he would have clipped our ear followed by a size ten boot up our backsides.

Our favourite object for this intelligent behaviour would be a cast-iron gas stove, the impact was like that of an exploding bomb. No boys were ever seriously injured by these capers, but now and again some boy would be in the wrong place at the wrong time.

Johnny Nunston was such a boy. He was a horrible kid always telling his mum on us. You know the type, had a face not unlike Mick Jagger, big fat lips, shouted his mouth off all the time. If we played cricket in the street, if anyone caught him out, he would storm off home, taking his ball with him just to ruin the game for the rest of us. In short a right little toad.

Nobody wanted Johnny Nunston on their side in any of the mock battles we played together. These battles were so dangerous, raiding each others camps, using stones and slates as missiles, raining these down on our enemy, our only protection being a dustbin lid used like a medieval knight's shield. Clang, bang went the stones, zing, swish went the house slates skimming like non-returnable boomerangs, head-height from house to house, window to window.

Johnny Nunston and boys unfortunate enough to be on his side, were one day pinned down on the first floor of the big completely bombed-out house on the corner of Camden Grove.

We of course on the conquering army had battered them into a no-escape situation, but they intended to fight to the last man. They always did that in the pictures didn't they? Their defensive position seemed impregnable. Until Jimmy volunteered for a suicide mission, creeping forward to enable himself to be under the large first floor window yet still completely unseen by Commander J Nunston, who up until now had been making regular appearances at the window, shouting insults at our brave army. He would disappear just as quickly before a volley of brick, stones, and chunks of wood could get him.

This had been going on for some time when Jimmy, in his position far below and unseen by Johnny Nunston, lobbed a whole house brick with all his might at the open window above.

The brick seemed to fly as if in slow motion—up, up—in a gentle curve. As we boys watched,

Johnny Nunston made his final appearance at the window with a sneering 'you can't get me' on his fat blubbery lips still being spoken, the house brick landed flat on his face. It by now had lost most of its momentum so Johnny was saved from any serious injury, but the cheers from our army could be heard for miles. We stormed the building, Johnny ran home to tell his Mum on us once again, but I shall remember the look on 'Johnny the Toad's' face as long as I shall live, it was great.

These battles would sometimes result in a nasty cut or bump for some boy. Jimmy's younger brother Kenny still has a scar on the bridge of his nose. A boy in the distance sent a sheet of tin skimming in his direction, popping his head above the hide just as it flew overhead it caught him right between the eyes. He in his mid fifties now, with the scar to remind him of those battles still there.

It is important to remember we boys were living in the most violent time in history and quite naturally would role-play the events we would see on the newsreels at the cinema. But to us this was paradise. We could hate the Germans, confident we would win and in the meantime had more freedom for adventure than any boys ever had before.

Jimmy Hughes' father, a smashing man, also a James, was a very active member of the Home Guard. Ddressed in his ill-fitting battledress, he would regularly parade with his comrades in the streets of Peckham. An odd assortment of men very determined to do their bit for England if the dreaded Nazi hoards ever tried to invade Peckham. Men of all ages made up their ranks, each one in their minds a fierce fighter.

One wonders what Hitler's crack infantry would have made of them if they had seen them as I did one Saturday afternoon, creeping in a column one behind the other, ducking into doorways as if under attack in Rye Lane, a busy shopping street in Peckham. Each man holding onto his wooden cutout of a rifle, which at the barrel end dangled a string of fire crackers.

With great dramatic acting from Dad's Army soldiers, they would pull the string when simulating firing the wooden gun—each pull produced a small bang. Darting in and out of the doorways, bumping into shoppers tripping over each other in their anxiety to appear very war like indeed. This produced much laughter from the busy shoppers as they tried desperately to keep out of their way.

Eventually, when well equipped, the Home Guard became a force to be reckoned with. Fortunately their resolve would never have to be tested as the tide had turned against Hitler. And, as the threat subsided, our hopes for an early successful end to the war soared.

Great news ... Germany was losing the war. We were confident that the combined power of the British, US and allied forces would crush Hitler and the Nazi party very soon now. How soon was impossible to say. The landings in France had been successful, yet Hitler's new weapon the V1 flying bomb, or doodle bug as we called it, was creating terrible fear in London and the South East of England.

When the first V1 came over London no one believed that it was a pilotless plane. To us that was impossible, a plane without a pilot... unbelievable. They were first reported as an aircraft on fire, due to the flames spouting from the exhaust stack. The unforgettable pop-pop roar they emitted as they flew quite low over the blackened chimney pots of London before they stopped with an eerie silence, followed seconds later by an enormous explosion as the 1,900lb warheads blasted what was left of our City into further piles of rubble.

Thousands of these doodle bugs came over, Hitler thinking his last-ditch terror weapon would enable him to end the war with some form of terms, thus saving his neck. We certainly had not gone this far to allow that to happen. We British dived into our shelters as usual as soon as we heard them coming, then carried on as normal until the next pop, pop roar from the engines drew our eyes to the sky.

Will this one go over, mother thought, as she grabbed me by the coat one day in just such a situation. We had just left Len Buxton's corner grocer shop, our weeks meagre ration in our rexin carrier bag, splutter, splutter, then the engine stopped, we were lucky. At the entrance of the Camden Arms Public House close by was a sandbag-protected entrance to the bar.

In a matter of seconds mother had dragged me into the safety of the shelter. It was then I heard the loudest explosion of the war. It was enormous. The blast combined with the showers of debris which flashed down the street. a thick black cloud formed a few streets away. Rushing home happy that this one also did not have our name on it. Oh well, not to worry, by now we were battle-hardened Londoners.

What's on the wireless and who's pinched my Beano comic suddenly became more important subjects to me than Hitler—who only has one ball, Goebbel's hasn't any at all (words from a song sang at school by we boys in 1940). The doodle bugs continued to plague London for many months to come and 121 Peckham Road really did have some near misses.

The nearest one and I certainly would not like it to have been much closer, was late one evening when Dad and I were standing at our front door during a raid. The sirens had sounded, we should have taken cover but as Hitler had given up sending planes over we felt quite safe watching the regular arrival of the doodle bugs. They would fly over, the flames from their exhausts having a fascination. We felt that as we could see them we had a better chance to take cover at the last minute, rather than the blanket bombing we had experienced for so many years, trapped for hours as the bombs rained down in their thousands.

This doodle bug came out of the half light straight at us. We could see it as a dot at first, the familiar rumble of its engine quite faint in the distance. As it grew close, the black bulk of its warhead in the centre of its short square tipped wings came into view. We both had the horrible feeling that we could read in bold white chalk the words Parsons, 121 Peckham Road.

It was impossible to see any flames from its exhaust as its angle was straight at us. To our horror its engine cut out, it started its dive. From where we were it was heading for the front door. Dad and I made a dash for the narrow staircase leading to our shelter.

'This is our lot,' he yelled as a warning to my mother and sister Jean below in the shelter.

I was in the shelter, when Dad in his haste fell headlong down the stairs behind me. An almighty boom followed a blast that made the house shake to its foundations. We could not believe the house was still standing. Once again we had been lucky. The V1 flying bomb, Hitler's secret weapon, had found its target at the end of Camden Grove, demolishing a whole block near the Bradford Hall Boys' Club, frequently used by the local boys for sporting activities. We had escaped the whole incident safely, except for Dad's back that was badly bruised from his fall down the staircase.

The V1 flying bomb with all its accompanying terror lasted for many months and just when we all felt that they had ended and we would be safe at last from that madman Adolph Hitler, he used his final terror weapon on us. This really was the most awful monster, a silent monster that fell from the sky, not only without a pilot but this time unseen and worst of all unheard. The V2 attacks had started, the ultimate weapon, impossible to intercept, impossible for us to take shelter from, they just fell from the sky on a clear blue day, smashing a defenceless city once more.

Our family had one near miss from one of these black and white painted rockets. Granddad George having survived being blown out of his lorry at hell fire corner in World War One, the Germans nearly managed to kill him once again as he innocently travelled on the top deck of a tram travelling along the New Cross Road. His tram had just passed the Woolworth Store in New Cross when suddenly it was there no more.

Looking back from his vantage point on the top deck of the tram he told me there was nothing but smoke, debris raining down everywhere. If his tram had been a few seconds earlier he would have been at the centre of the explosion. Amazingly our family had been so lucky once again.

There was a terrible loss of life in the store as the attack happened during working hours on a busy Saturday. I seemed to be having so much fun at home now that the regular bombing raids at night had ended, we were allowed out quite late to rollerskate around the C & A Stores in Rye Lane.

This being the new craze we had formed the Skating Wanderers Club, printing our own passbooks, membership strictly restricted. But I had started to notice that Mum and Dad were far from being happy. Terrible rows were commonplace, unaware as a child that the two major problems in a marriage, sex and money, had obviously become major barriers for them.

Mum didn't like sex—she told me that when I was still quite young—and Dad did not like parting with his money. He would refuse to buy her anything unless she really put pressure on him, and I can guess exactly how she brought pressure on him. Pressure built in the home until one day mother left him. Mum, sister Jean and I arrived at Aunt Nance's flat complete with suitcases, mother vowing never to return to him again. I thought it was great, I loved staying there anyway.

Not many days passed before Dad arrived pleading with mother to return home. Dad was a great actor when he wanted to be, so here he was crying, throwing himself about in despair, showing great regret over his past behaviour. Realising that mother was not getting impressed, she had seen it all before, he turned to me with a forlorn look in his eyes.

'Wouldn't you like to come home with me, Freddie,' he said.

'Nope,' I said. 'I just love it here.'

Those forlorn eyes darkened to angry black, flashed at me then returned to mother for a further attempt. I always felt rotten about saying that to him, but I was enjoying our stay at Auntie's home, his final effort to win Mum came as he threw himself down a full flight of stairs making sure he bumped down every step on his bottom crying bitterly.

The crying stopped surprisingly suddenly as mother said, 'Alright, I will come home.'

Back home mother was riding high for a while. Dad was a new man, he had given her a hundred pounds for her own bank account, promised to take her to a show in the West End of London once every month, promised not to tell lies any more. He had been an habitual liar since a boy. Granddad Parsons said he was so bad they would not believe him over anything. 'Should have beaten it out of him as a kid,' he was heard to say to mother when she confided in Granddad over his lying problem. He would tell real whoppers for really no reason whatsoever.

It took just one trip to a West End show for Dad to find reasons to back out of his new resolutions. He tried to get his money back. desperately pleading to Mum that he only lent her the hundred pounds and he needed it back. She made sure he never did get his hands on her hard fought-for cash.

He refused to take her anywhere after that, so she only saw one show. The atmosphere deteriorated back to as it was before, total lack of love between them. If there was not much love at this time, there definitely was some sex, probably used by Mum on a points basis to get what she needed in return.

High on our mantelpiece stood an oak cigarette box that when you lifted the lid up popped a cigarette, quite a novelty at the time. Dad had fitted an old car clock into the centre of the box. It had stood there for many years ticking away, until one day on my own with nothing to occupy my mind, I flipped the lid open on the box.

Oops, much to my surprise, on the little tray that normally raised the cigarette to the top of the box, popped a large condom rolled in the usual way, teat hanging limply over the end. Taking this out of the box for further examination, I recognised what it was straight away from the many times I had seen similar balloons like these hanging on the gorse bushes at Epson after the Yanks had walked out with their girlfriends, unaware of our prying eyes.

Yet this one was different. A horrible pale yellow and as

thick as a bicycle inner tube, it was a washable condom. Trust Dad to get the most for his money, wash it leave it to dry, then you are ready to go again. I'm not surprised Mum was none too keen on sex. After close examination and a quick attempt to blow it up, I returned it to its hideaway.

Why the condom was in the clock, one can only assume that the living room was the warmest place in our house in winter. Probably another reason for mother's reluctance to respond to Dad's ardent overtures was his hatred of water, he just would not bath.

Mother would never bother all year, but as Christmas grew near, she would plead with him, 'Fred you are going to have a bath for Christmas.'

'Yes, yes,' he would snap back.

This would go on for some weeks until her final demand would be answered with, 'Oh, didn't I tell you I had one while you were out.'

So once again he had avoided water. He also hated any cold air getting to his body. When he did finally change his underclothes, this was always done late at night, his clean longjohns, vest, shirt, all laid out around the fire to warm up, before a sudden change over was done. That would last him for quite some weeks before he needed to repeat the unpleasant process.

Dad always slept in his shirt and vest and in the winter probably his longjohns as well. He would wear longjohns summer or winter. As an extra comforter in winter in bed at night, he would wrap an old pullover around his head. He said his head became cold and this kept him warm. Dad was of small stature, very bony, looked seventy five years old when he was only twenty eight. Can you imagine the sight that met mother's eyes when she entered her bedroom?

There was Fred, short and bony with his shirt and

longjohns on, a jumper wrapped around his head, had not bathed for years, saying 'who's for sex tonight, darling?'

It's not surprising that she was not too keen is it?

CHAPTER FOURTEEN

THE GREAT SHELTER SHOW

The war was very nearly at its end now, Hitler was cornered up in his bunker about to take his last breath, no more raids on London, just the bombed remains of a once beautiful city. Everywhere you looked could be seen shattered shells of houses amazingly defying gravity by still standing there, we boys still using them as our adventure playground. The shelters now no longer needed as a bolt hole for a terrified population became a new opportunity for us, an ideal spot to have meetings, our gang made great use of the large, brick free-standing shelter adjoining the Walmer Castle Pub.

One boy, obviously to become a great entrepreneur in later life, started to organise shows in this shelter on a regular basis. A small charge was asked for boys to enter. Our twelve year old entertainments manager promised that all our halfpenny entrance fees would be in aid of the Red Cross. I think that the contents of the tin box he used to collect his box office takings went towards his first Rolls Royce.

We would file into the shelter until all the bunk beds

were full with boys, their little white knees hanging over the edges of the beds, as boys scrambled for the higher bunks to get a better view of the show. Candles flickered from jam jars creating a stagelike atmosphere at one end of stark brick interior. The great shelter show was about to start.

A series of boys would stand up, walk to the candlelit improvised stage and tell the dirtiest joke they could think of. The Gillam brothers would tell of their latest idea for making 'lots of money'—they had found a ready market for scrap lead, so were systematically stripping the lead from the rooftops of bombed houses. One boy would play his mouth organ. Nobody could really make out what he was playing, but it all added to the atmosphere. Woodbine cigarettes would be removed from their pack of five in paper packets. A match would flash in the dark, followed by plumes of blue smoke wafting around the unventilated night club for boys. But this was only the forerunner to the big turn of the evening.

As we boys sat on our bunks, swinging our legs impatiently waiting for the real reason we had begrudgingly surrendered our halfpennies for at the door. Whispering went among us. She was definitely going to take it off wasn't she? We had all been told by our great shelter show host that TITSERLINA would top the bill and would without doubt show all. You can see now why the shelter was so full and the tin box so heavy for our entertainments manager to carry.

At last Titserlina made her appearance looking as full-bodied as we had all remembered her. She smiled at the rows of little faces, mouths open in anticipation. Without saying a word she started to unbutton her blouse. The silence in the shelter was eerie. I think we even all stopped breathing as well. The tension was so great you could hear the buttons click one by one. At last she undid the remaining button then, with a sweep of her arms, flicked her blouse back over her shoulders...wow!

Every boy there sucked in air at the same time, it is a wonder that the candles stayed alight with such a sudden consumption of oxygen. She stood there, obviously very fond of her beautiful breasts, and would only have sacrificed herself because of her desire to aid the Red Cross, I am sure.

I remember thinking it was the best value that a halfpenny had ever given me. I never ever knew her real name but that night she really lived up to her nickname of Titserlina.

The show being over our host addressed his audience, 'Boys, purely to aid the Red Cross, Titserlina will allow a further service to the show. Any boy that wishes to enter the booth as they leave...' the booth being a cubicle used for the chemical toilets, now removed.

Titserlina would allow any boy that wished to donate a halfpenny to the Red Cross fund, the pleasure of feeling her breasts. The frantic rattle of coins could be heard as boys checked their pockets for the necessary funds.

'Also,' continued our host, 'for those who are prepared to donate one penny she will allow you to feel her down below.'

Searching through my pockets I was delighted to find a halfpenny straight away, but search as hard as I could not one extra coin could I find. I joined the end of the line of boys shuffling slowly towards the booth for what seemed like ages.

I eventually found myself outside the sacking entrance, our entertainments manager rattled his tin at me. 'Up the top or down the bottom?' he asked.

Dropping my halfpenny into his tin box, I sadly said, 'Only on the top.'

Moving forward under the sack, hands outstretched, palms forward, it was so dark I could see virtually nothing. My hands came in contact with two beautiful warm smooth melons, a quick squeeze and out of the booth I went, happy in the knowledge that they felt as wonderful as they looked. On my way home that night I daydreamed of what could have been if only I had had that extra halfpenny on me—ah well.

Peckham had become so peaceful now, no danger at all from the enemy, everything still in short supply though. Spivs—the name given to black market salesmen, who would always obtain anything you needed, were everywhere. They would stand on street corners, trilby hats pulled down over their eyes…

'Knicker elastic, lady, only sixpence a yard, can't buy it anywhere else love…' and they were right. Elastic was very difficult to find in shops.

'Nylons, darling—just your size, go on, girl, give the old man a treat tonight…' their small suitcase held out in front of them had it all.

Shifty eyes and always a small pencil-thin moustache, head regularly popping up above the crowd watching for a policeman's approach—The Spiv, but a loveable rogue.

It was shortly after this period that I tasted my first banana for five years provided by just such a Spiv at 6d each. We ate quite a few, enjoying the forgotten taste from pre-war days. Ice cream made a happy return to our lives, on sale at the black and white milk bar in Rye Lane, Peckham. These milk bars were very popular as meeting places for young people, a forerunner to the coffee bars, named black and white milk bars because of the black and white-tiled interiors.

My little sister Jean had now entered show business. Mother had become very involved with a children's dancing class club. Jean being cute and mother a good dressmaker, made a good combination for the amateur shows that were produced on quite a regular basis, using local halls, most of the audience made up of parents and friends of the children.

Jean would practice every night at home to perfect her par bars and shuffle tap dancing steps. Mother would spend hours hammering away at her sewing machine making outfits for the whole cast, a new material now available called plastic, smelt awful, had a waxy feel to it, came in bright fluorescent colours though that made it ideal for stage outfits.

Jean looked just like Peckham's answer to Shirley Temple, wearing a large bonnet hat, a tiny short skirt, big ribbon bows on her tap shoes, all in fluorescent red plastic. It is a wonder that mother's sewing machine never caught fire from the hard work it did producing all these outfits.

Feeling a little left out of all the glamour going on around me, I confided in Mum that I envied the only boy in the all girl dancing group.

'You have a beautiful voice,' mother said. 'You could be the lead singer in no time, if you tried.'

Mothers always overrate their son's abilities, mine was no exception. I should have remembered the time she talked me into having my hair permed. Looking back I am surprised I finished up normal at all.

No more than a week had passed by before I walked into Barbara Craw's Juveniles Dancing School, complete with brand new black patent dancing shoes. No, she had not made me a skirt yet, but I did have a smart pair of black long trousers, my hair slicked down flat and shining with an application of Brylcream. My heart sank as I entered the hall full of giggling girls, hovered over by doting mothers.

Jean ran over and joined the line-up for the chorus. The principles and only boy stood in the middle of this bevy of bony-kneed beauties, the piano struck up a few chords and off they went into a high-kicking tap number.

I cringed in acute embarrassment. Oh, what a sissy he looked, dancing there, kicking his legs in the air with all those girls. I knew straight away this was not going to be for me, but having come this far I felt I really could not back out yet.

'I hear he can sing quite well,' said Barbara Craws, a short dark-haired woman in her fifties, a very bossy lady, obviously an old show business has-been, her very timid hen pecked husband cringed at the piano waiting for every signal.

Taking me by the elbow she walked me into the centre of the hall and up to the piano. 'He's going to sing Apple Blossom Time,' she snapped at the unfortunate Mr Craws.

'What key?' enquired Mr Craws, 'would you like to sing in?'

'I don't know,' said I. 'I just sing.'

I had never thought about the key, my face was flushing to an embarrassed scarlet, facing me was the smirking face of the principle boy, obviously delighting in my confusion and determined to hate me even more if I sang well.

After various notes up and down the scale were hammered on the piano and a few squeaky sounds from me until something near enough was reached.

'You start and I'll follow,' said Mr Craws.

'I'll be with you in apple blossom time,' came from my trembling lips.

Mother smiled and purred her approval, the cringing

pianist tried hard to keep with me, the pasty face little sissy did his best to put me off by smirking at me the whole time. At last the torture ended, a flutter of patronising claps could be heard as I made my hasty exit.

'Very nice,' said the principle boy's mother, not meaning a word of it.

Her son said nothing at all to me. If only I could have knocked that silly smirk off his face the whole evening would have been worthwhile.

On the way home mother was furious.

'I don't care, I am never going to classes again,' I said 'They are for sissies.'

The black patent tap shoes stood for many weeks after that on top of the wardrobe, as new, unmarked, still with the one pound fifty pence sticker on them. So endeth my show business career for some years anyway. Later my desire for the spotlight showed itself again, when as an adult I would train dogs for TV.

Parsons car hire had become very busy, Dad had started to employ part time drivers because so many servicemen had decided to get married, weddings were big business at weekends, the war was nearly over and everyone felt safe at last, so the desire to take the plunge was on, wedding bookings were regular, Dad had the cars for the job, things were really looking up for him.

We were still visiting Regma, the bad feeling generated by selling the car to Tommy Reeves had been forgotten by now, Ma was her old jolly self, house full of stable lads as usual. I had started to stay at Mrs Ashes on weekends, that shows what a forgiving lady she was. Helping out at Johnny Dines Racing Stables, was the big attraction again. I still felt that I might make a jockey, if only I did not grow too big. The dusty hut was still going strong.

'Would you like to come with us tonight?' said Mum.

Great thought I, as it would give me a chance to show off my new double breasted brown pinstripe suit mother had bought me from a spiv.

'No coupons, lady, just a bit dusty it is.'

Dusty it certainly was, probably looted from some shop after an air raid it was thick with plaster dust, but with a lot of brushing and a press it looked really smart. Dressed in my new suit I really felt I was jack the lad. I sauntered around the dusty hut feeling very grown up, making frequent visits to the men's toilet to admire myself and slick back the quiff in my Brylcreamed hair. It was embarrassing to dance with one's mother on occasions like this.

One, two, three, one, two three, I kept saying to myself as we slowly moved around the dusty floor. I hope nobody notices who I am dancing with I thought to myself.

Although my head was buried into mother's chest, she being quite a lot taller than me at the time, out of the corner of my eye I spotted a pretty face looking straight at me, I remembered her at once, it was Cathy Reedman, looking very grown up and quite beautiful. What an awful time to see her again, dancing with your mum, not the image I wanted to portray at all. That whole evening I gazed at her yet never had the courage to say a word. She would look back at me and smiled many times.

My mind drifted back to memories of the time we walked home from school together, that grassy bank...

'Ladies and Gentlemen, the last waltz please,' called the master of ceremonies.

Out on the dance floor I went, face into mother's chest once more. 'Who's taking you home tonight' crooned the singer on the stage. My Mum, thought I. Oh, I wish I could be really grown up. As the revellers noisily left the dusty hut that night I looked for a glimpse of Cathy, but she was gone. Walking back to Regma that night I could think of nothing else except Cathy Reedman, my hormones must really have been boiling that night.

The sleepy Village of Langley Bottom with all its interesting characters had not changed. The tiny petrol station on the corner with its tall upright pump, the corrugated iron green painted school on the hill. The strings of racehorses clip clopping their way back from the downs after their exercise, racing lads on their backs spinning their whips through their fingers with professional ease, their knees high in the stirrups resting on sweating beautiful thoroughbreds, their coats burnished to a golden chestnut from weeks of dedicated care, a wonderful sight on a spring morning with the mist still on the downs.

So this was the Langley Bottom I had loved so much. The Ash family that had protected me and tolerated me, would be there for many years to come. I would remember them all with so much love and affection. Snowy always a bit deaf, hand to his ear, his bright blue eyes smiling at you always. Was he really having an affair with the woman on the hill, well it was a juicy scandal anyway. Beatie, the little dwarf lady who always looked so sad, Tommy Reeves, whose black wavy hair I coveted so much, Hobo, who still looked like a tramp and all the rest of their family that made Regma such a happy place to be.

I can only share my story with you—these people were unaware of the happy memories they were helping to create for a little boy. And Ma, that courageous and loving lady—I shall always remember her in her blue air raid warden's uniform galloping around Tattenham Corner, steel helmet wobbling, pitting her very stalwart self against Hitler's might. With English ladies like her he didn't stand a chance.

I shall remember the tears in her eyes when I entered her bedroom to find her sad and tearful, holding the photo of her little girl who died so very young. She was unable to leave her room all afternoon, the memory of her daughter's death was so painful for her. She was a wonderful homemaker, life at Regma centred around her it was an unbelievably happy place.

A very special lady, I am happy to say Ma lived to a ripe old age, living at Regma with her loving sons around her until the end. Beatie died only a few years after I left Epsom. Her eldest son after five years at war in Burma was killed in a train accident within one year of his return. Thirty years later, on a visit to Langley Bottom in 1975, the spirit of Ma was still there for me, but standing at her gate was a grey-haired man.

I hesitantly approached. 'Are you Ron Ash?' I asked.

'Yes,' was his reply.

'It's me, Freddie Parsons,' I said, expecting instant recognition.

'Ah yes,' was his response, after very slow deliberation, then he said nothing.

Ron, Ma's fourth son had forgotten me. I walked away happy that Regma still had its name on the gate and that there still was an Ash family living there. But sad for me because it was all gone now, only my memories are left to transport me back to hear the sights and sounds of Regma with all my characters full of life filling the house with laughter, the Regma I loved in the 1940s.

Mum and Dad's visits to Epsom became fewer and fewer until they eventually lost touch with the Ash family, as is the way in life. I started to become involved with planning what I should do when I left school at fourteen—pardon, what was that I heard you say—I didn't tell you what happened to Cathy Reedman. You don't want to hear any more about my exploits with Cathy do you? You do, you do, oh well, here goes then, don't blame me if it's too racy for you.

As you will remember Cathy was very much on my mind after the dusty hut dance. Much to my delight a few weekends later I saw Cathy's appealing shape high on the hill standing next to the red telephone box on the pathway leading to the downs. Hurrying as fast as I could to get there before she disappeared I slowed the last few paces to appear more relaxed.

'Hello, Cathy,' I said. 'It's so nice to see you again,' hoping that my innocent boyish charm hid my true intentions.

We talked for some time with my mind whirling, this was my opportunity to redeem myself in Cathy's eyes, to say nothing of the good time I hoped to get.

'Oh, you're on your way home'—that little devil sitting on my shoulder shouting at me, go boy go—'I'll walk with you then.' said I, knowing there was an awful lot of grassy banks on the way.

A short while later found Cathy and I kissing in the long grass. Magic moments were exchanged that afternoon and as in all good love stories we will fade out the picture at this point. Remember this is in 1945, so you can't expect too much detail can you. Let me say this to you though, Cathy did not storm off that afternoon, so at last I must have been doing something right.

CHAPTER FIFTEEN

VE DAY PARTY

The war is over—those wonderful few words we had been waiting to hear for six years were now headlines in the newspaper. Hitler is dead, Germany has surrendered. The evil Nazi regime has gone forever. The people were ecstatic with joy, loved ones would be returning home at last, as the wartime song said—there really would be blue birds flying over the white cliffs of Dover at last.

We hugged each other with joy, our family had survived the war, we were so lucky there had not been a bomb somewhere with our name on it after all. So many other families, the joy was tainted by the bitterness of lost loved ones, but this was a time to rejoice. An official Victory in Europe date was declared by Winston Churchill, our wonderful wartime prime minister, celebrations were being organised everywhere. Our contribution was to be a street party held in East Surrey Grove.

The large area that Hitler had flattened with one of his bombs made a perfect area to lay out dozens of tables end to end, we boys worked hard for days clearing and flattening the ground, bricks were laid in rows to edge out the boundary to the tables, it was to be a very grand affair, the adults had organised themselves into a V.E. party group. We boys not to be outdone. After all it was our bomb site they were using, organised a boys' own committee.

Jimmy Hughes, Norman Banfield, were the leaders, we other kids being the small fry. A lot depended on your age, the younger kids being given the really rotten jobs. Little Johnny Buxton being only eight years old at the time would probably have been given a really awful job had it not been for the fact that his dad owned Len's Corner Grocery Shop, so we all felt it was a very good idea to keep in with him, any boy that had a father in total control of a sweetshop, had my friendship for life. As it turned out that is just what actually happened. John has been a dear friend all my life, a kinder more genuine man would be impossible to find. We have shared many of life's adventures together. He has been and will always be like a brother to me.

Johnny Nunston, the sneeky snidy little toad of a boy with lips like Mick Jagger would have been given something really dangerous in the hope that he would fall in or fall off something. We all enjoyed seeing Johnny Nunston get hurt, he was always screaming for his mum over nothing at all, so when he really had a reason such as the time he walked into the house brick that Jimmy Hughes tossed through the open window, we all cheered like mad.

For days before the party we collected absolutely any object that would burn from every bombed house in the streets around our area, doors, window frames, any old furniture left behind by the unfortunate inhabitants. Floorboards were torn up, roof rafters torn down until we had the most enormous pile, stacked so high it was impossible to reach the top without ladders. This was going to be the bonfire of all bonfires. East Surrey Grove was being decorated, anything that had red white and blue on it was removed from attics, dusted off and displayed from our window. We were so proud and happy and quite rightly so. The Germans under the Nazi Party thought they could conquer and enslave us, yes, we had beaten them and we were proud of it.

The morning the big day arrived filling us full of excitement, we boys were out first thing, attending to all the last minute details. Our bomb site had never looked so smart with its rows of white painted bricks giving a neat boundary to the party area. Tables arriving from everywhere being joined together to form a huge banqueting table, starched white table cloths hiding the joins until they become one great table spanning the whole of the area, masses of crockery appeared as if from nowhere to fill the table with settings. Mothers arrived carrying every imaginable delicacy, jellies and cakes filled the tables to overflowing, spam sandwiches, their revolting rubbery contents spewing from hundreds of neatly cut squares filling plates to gravity defying heights.

Forms and chairs were arranged around the main table. We kids could hardly bare the tension as the minutes ticked away before the banquet was to start. It was at this moment that I noticed near the top of the main table to the left was a small table all on its own and separate, being about six foot away from the main group, neatly laid out with white table cloths and plate settings for about four people.

It was not until the mad rush was on as we children stormed the tables intent on devouring all the food in sight within seconds, that I realised who would sit at the small table. Would you believe it, Jimmy Hughes, Norman Banfield and two other boys had arranged their own table for the boys' committee only.

I was furious, the rotters. I had worked really hard on all the preparation only to be left out at the last minute from a place of honour at their table. I can still remember how angry I felt as I stuffed rock cakes into my mouth as fast as I could. Here I was sitting on the big table with dozens of other kids who did nothing towards preparing our bomb site for the party while their Lordships sat in style smugly bathing in all the thanks for their efforts.

If looks could kill there would have been four dead kids slumped over that table that afternoon.

We all ate so much food that day that we could hardly leave the table, Mums and Dads endlessly replacing empty plates with full ones, the ladies entering into the festive mood had dressed in fancy dress outfits.

Jimmy Hughes' mother wore a black and white checked cockney barrow boy's costume with large cap set at a jaunty angle. My mother wore a gypsy dress with bandana around her hair and very dangling hooped earrings. The tea party over, we children played around in the street or on the bomb site as usual, our parents had arranged the use of a hall on the opposite side of the street to where our V.E. party was being held.

A scouts' hall called by the unusual name of 'the Pit Street Settlement', outside the house adjoining the hall was a shrine to the Virgin Mary that was always illuminated by a red glowing light. The owner of the house and the scouts' hall was an eccentric old man named Major Watson, a tall upright man with grey hair a veteran of the first world war.

He founded the settlement and was chief scout of the 6th Camberwell Scouting Branch, having lost a leg in World War One, he fascinated us boys with his steel leg that clicked as he walked in his boy scouts' shorts, one steel leg showing, his four cornered scouts' hat on, waving his walking stick high as though he was going over the top of the trenches in France. He would frighten the life out of us boys, most of the local lads had joined his scout troop or had been in the cubs at some time.

He was a bachelor, lived on his own with a housekeeper, would invite you in to see his many trophies that he had collected from Africa, gave us some sweets from a large tin always on his sideboard, had the irritating habit of sitting you on his knee, the steel one, grabbing you under the armpits, lifting you up and then slamming you down again as hard as he could on his very hard mechanical leg. Roaring with laughter as he did it to you, appearing completely oblivious to the pain it was causing.

Hmm, looking back on his behaviour, I have my doubts about Major Watson, but in fairness to him he never did anything that at the time we felt was more than just boisterous high spirits.

It was very kind of him to allow this hall to be used for the evening celebrations, as the neighbours filed in he looked very smart in his uniform smelling of moth balls but brushed and pressed to perfection, his medals gleaming proudly on his chest it must have been a great day for the old war horse.

'Come in, come in, dear ladies,' giving us all a welcoming greeting in his refined very upper class accent. Why the old major would be living in East Surrey Grove in Peckham, a very working class area still quite baffles me, but there he was very much like our very own squire of the manor with his serfs tipping their hats to him on passing in the street with 'Good morning, Major'.

He really was a colourful character, he lived in the same house for the rest of his life until sadly the whole area was demolished, replaced by hideous new flats totally lacking in style and character. It's hard to believe now that in 1945 it was so safe to walk the streets, that people would leave their front doors keys dangling inside their letter boxes on a long piece of string to enable the children to reach in and open their door with the key.

Inside the hall that night the live three piece band blasted out the music of the time, Glen Miller's 'In the Mood', a popular favourite, the older people sliding across the floor doing the quickstep being constantly irritated by the younger revellers' gyrations as they performed the near acrobatics of the jitterbugging, one of those new-fangled dances taught to the British population by Hollywood Films and the US servicemen here helping to fight the loneliness of our local girls.

Oak barrels of dark beer were stacked in rows on trestle tables, the wooden taps being constantly turned as pint glass after pint glass was filled to the brim, as the barrels got lower the laughter got louder, the band by now was as drunk as the party goers, blasting out one hot tune after another until the party was nearly raising the roof off the scouts' hall.

Outside in the darkened street we kids played games popping into the hall for the occasional lemonade, on one corner house next to the Camden Arms Pub, some old dears had managed to drag a large upright piano onto their front garden and were bashing out the old favourites— 'Sweet Aderline', 'It's a long way to Tipperary', 'My old man said follow the van', all the really good numbers sung with great gusto, even if the piano had most of its keys producing bum notes.

The moment came for us at last to light the bonfire, rag was wrapped around a pole, impregnated with paraffin, bursting into flames and burning brightly illuminating our expectant faces, flames started to flicker then licking quickly up the sides of the bonfire as it started to burn, within minutes the flames were roaring into the black night sky. It burnt so brightly and for so long that night turned into day, unlike all the other fires that we had endured as London burned from Nazi bombing for six long years, this fire filled us with happiness.

As the fire illuminated the remaining houses in East Surrey Grove, music and laughter filled the streets, no longer would the cries from smoking rubble bring neighbours rushing from their shelters, searching for loved ones buried beneath tons of bricks, timber and dust. But soon these remaining little houses would disappear to another tyrant.

So-called progress, in place of the warm and friendly little homes, with their gardens filled with hollyhocks. Each with its large tin bath hanging on its rear garden wall waiting for Friday nights' ritual. Where neighbours, new neighbours, families lived and died for generations together, before pesticides killed everything that moved in our gardens. An environment where spiders, so big they could not turn around in a match box, sat in the middle of their huge webs glistening with morning dew. A place where, even in wartime, children were safe to play in the streets, old ladies found teenagers caring and helpful, perverts, muggers, rapists, murderers—they did not exist in our world.

Murder would be headlines in a daily paper, it was a safe and honest society in 1945. As that generation passes on they must be very sad to see life as it is in 1993.

Yes, they tore down the little houses, slums they called them. What we needed was new streets in the sky, our own bathroom.

'No need for the tin bath now,' said these experts on how we should live, thinking they could design a correct way of life for us simply by putting a pen to a drawing board. Down they came by their thousands, achieving in months what Lord Haw Haw and the Luftwaffer had taken years to do.

In their place came the high rise flats, floor after floor of characterless dwellings. Neighbours never meet neighbours anymore, lifts are urinated in by mindless vandals, at night it's not safe to leave your flat for fear of being mugged, perverts are out there looking for a chance to molest or even murder your children. No longer does a row between neighbours end with a bloody nose. Today you are lucky if you get to intensive care before you die from knife wounds. That is the society of the 1990s.

But this night in 1945 from the bright light from our bonfire I could still see it all there. Len's corner shop, that always had the wonderful smell of ham on the bone freshly cooked in their own kitchen at the back of the shop, rows of biscuit tins with their glass top displaying their contents. Len the perfect shopkeeper, always jolly never without a cheeky and sometimes risqué remark to his customers.

'Can I do you now madam', 'very tasty very sweet', all lines from a radio show at the time called 'ITMA'. The star of the show, a comedian called Tommy Handley, was very famous and Len was our own happy chappie, a really delightful little man, who had the most understanding wife in the world Jessie.

On one occasion Len had been out on a binge with two friends, crawling from pub to pub until very late. They arrived back at his shop in the early hours of the morning. After banging on his door for some time, Len's wife got up from her bed to confront the revellers. Len in the middle supported either side by his friends was completely legless, his face was smothered from ear to ear in brilliant red lipstick kisses, dangling there limply between their arms, grinning with glazed eyes, he protested he had been attacked by these women in a pub that night.

Jessie Buxton was furious, but not with Len, she lambasted his two friends for leading Len astray. What a wonderful woman.

That night there was no need for street lamps still unused since before the war, dancing in the street the revellers illuminated by the brightness of the bonfire were really letting their hair down. Inside the Camden Arms Pub, Mrs Kicks the publican's stout and fearsome wife, strutted around the bar looking like an angry territorial robin in her bright red dress. Mr Wilday danced happily with his wife his indiscretions with the naughty lady in the corner house forgotten.

Inside the scouts' hall the M.C. stopped the band for an announcement. 'Ladies and Gentlemen, I am sure I speak for all of us when I say how grateful we are for all the effort that the ladies have tirelessly spent in making this victory party such a huge success.'

As each lady was ushered to the front of the stage a thunderous applause ripped through the hall. Mother followed Jimmy's mum, the M.C. put his arm around her shoulders, 'thank you, Winn', giving her a hug.

With that mother burst into tears, she left the stage sobbing, Mrs Hughes Jimmy's mother trying to console her. No one ever knew why she became so upset, she said she didn't even know herself. I feel it was a symptom of the sudden release of all those years of stress she had gone through in the war. It was all an emotional time, mind you she had been wafting back quite a few gins that night as well and gin did make her feel sad.

The party never really ended that night it just drifted on

into the early hours groups of very happy people stood around the glowing embers of the fire, reliving their past experiences, we all had stories about lucky escapes and sadness for those lost during the raids, huddling close to each other that night we all felt the comradeship that so strongly held us together during those war years, people would never feel that close ever again, we needed each other very much during that time, fear had jelled us together as one, it really was as Winston Churchill said— OUR FINEST HOUR.

Only one big event was left to mark the end of the war. That was the big parades and celebrations in London's City centre, Trafalgar Square. Lord Nelson looking down on us from his column would have been very proud of his fellow Britons, as thousands and thousands of us filled his square to mark the official Victory in Europe Day. Mother had taken me there in the evening to experience this moment in history, it felt as though the whole population of London was there that night. Dancing and kissing each other in the square, the crowds moved about like the currents of the sea, gathering you up and swirling you about at its will.

The noise from the revellers was quite amazing, singing and cheering echoed around the tall elegant building in a musical ribbon of sound rising and falling constantly but never ending. So it was over we had won, right had been might in the end, we felt no sadness for the thousands and thousands of innocent Germans that had died by following a tyrant, it was our hour of glory, they had sown the wind and reaped the whirlwind, mother took me by the hand as we walked back down the Mall, one last look at Buckingham Palace before the No 12 bus took us back to 121 Peckham Road, all was quiet now, far too quiet for me I am afraid, I had lost my paradise of war.

My story now told—it leaves me with a tear in my eye and a lump in my throat for the characters in my story that are now no longer with us, but to be sad would not be what they would have wanted. They were all part of my moment in time, and they would have been pleased that I shared it with you.

My weather vane. The Spitfire once more driving the Messerschmitt 109 from our skies

The Battle of Britain Memorial at Dover. A very emotional and interesting place to visit

Spitfire awaiting takeoff at the Shuttleworth Collection Airshow, 1993

Manston Battle of Britain Museum. Superbly restored
Spitfire from Jimmy Corbin's Squadron

Manston Battle of Britain Museum. Hawker Hurricane, in
the hands of Ronald Kellett and Michael Ingle-Finch, an
outstanding fighting machine

Ronald Kellett's 85th birthday lunch. My wife, Beryl,
cutting his birthday cake

Michael Ingle-Finch, Beryl, Pam and Freddie enjoying
lunch and wartime nostalgia

CHAPTER SIXTEEN

FACE TO FACE WITH MY HEROES

Well, it's not the end of my story quite yet. Some fifty three years have passed since my story of 'One Boy's Heroes'. Fifty three years of thinking such admiration for those days when our brave boys fought the Hun high in the skies over Southern England.

How much we owed to them, they who died on those bright sunny days in 1940. The sadness and despair brought to these young men's families by that dreaded telegram or letter from their commanding officer, their brave and unflinching determination to destroy an invader utterly ruthless in his conviction that we should all be enslaved to Nazi Germany.

As children, my generation, was the last to remember the wartime spirit of the people of our great island. Because we are now too getting older, it is for us to remind the young of the great sacrifice that these brave men gave so that Great Britain should once again stay free.

1993—again on a hot summer's day a Spitfire engine burst into life with a huge blast of blue smoke from the exhausts of its Rolls Royce Merlin engine, set against the beautiful back cloth of the manicured airfield of the Shuttleworth

Vintage Aircraft Collection at Biggleswade. The Spitfire looked superb in its wartime camouflage colouring its engine purring with expectant power as it taxies for take off, the pilot in his light grey flying suit waved to the admiring crowd, then flying helmet on, he opens the throttles of the powerful 12 cylinder engine, the spine tingling roar as the worlds most beautiful fighter plane speeds down the run way sent a murmur of approval from the watching crowd as the aircraft became airborne and then banked sharply to speed low over the crowd at treetop height.

My thoughts at once went back to 1940 and the day the pilot of that other Spitfire after the deadly battle in the skies above Kent flew and victory-rolled his fighter almost within touching distance above us. His Spitfire unlike the shining sparkling restored beautiful airplane above us now, was oil-streaked and in dull chipped camouflage. A hot fighting machine made for war, inside that small cockpit sat a young man, whose destiny whether he would live or die only history would tell.

It was at this moment that as I looked and remembered the Spitfire of long ago, the desire to make contact and to thank personally the pilot that I admired so much grew in my mind. It was as if I was still looking into that September sky of 1940 hoping that the Ghost aircraft would roar overhead once more and with a wave of his wings make contact with me again. This time it would be for me to make contact with him a man possible in his late seventies perhaps living in the Kent area.

How would he react to a total stranger seeking his symbolic hero. He may find it very difficult to accept and understand my sincere feelings to hold out my hand and say from the bottom of my heart 'Thank you for all you did in 1940'.

Would he understand my need to thank him, would he understand the part he played in boosting our resolve in blitzed London to take all that Hitler could throw at us. I had to take that chance, I would seek him out, ask questions and hope for few rebuffs.

A few days later found me with the telephone in hand.

'Yes, this is Biggin Hill,' the famous fighter airfield had answered my call.

'Can I speak to Mr Jock Maitland,' I enquired.

Hesitantly, Jock Maitland, Spitfire pilot and now director of an air display team, came to the telephone. I had been told he might help me contact a Battle of Britain fighter pilot, now I had the awful job of explaining my reasons quickly and coldly over the telephone to a total stranger, at the same time trying desperately not to appear as some crank.

A very military and somewhat cold voice barked over the phone, 'Maitland here.'

My heart sank, confidence drained from my voice as I clumsily tried to explain my reasons for contacting this man. After a very stony start to my conversation he seemed to warm to me, my confidence soared allowing my sincere feelings to come through to this now very helpful man.

Yes, he would give me the names of not one but four Battle of Britain pilots, he understood my reasons and I like to think he was quite touched by them. I thanked him and was delighted to have got off to such a great start and to have spoken to such a nice man as Squadron Leader Jock Maitland.

I now had in front of me four names each of which was a total stranger. One by one I would contact them, but with the awesome task of explaining my reasons. Rejection was my biggest fear, for that would hurt me. These men were my boyhood heroes, but to them I would be just a voice on the telephone. I needed a further reason to call them … a party, a Battle of Britain party, they could be our guests of honour.

I would do just that, I would invite my old school friends, make it a really special occasion, we could all wallow in wartime nostalgia.

So a date was fixed as near as possible to the Battle of Britain Memorial Day, 15th September, and invitations were sent out to friends and family. Now with much intrepidation I would make contact with my fighter pilot.

Group Captain Darley DSO DFC
Battle of Britain fighter pilot, 609 Squadron, Spitfires

As my fingers punched out his telephone number my mind felt a total blank as to what to say, here I was again trying to find the magic phrase that would explain in a sentence my reasons for contacting him.

The very quiet gentle voice that answered my call immediately put me at ease. Explaining that, at eighty years of age, parties were not something that he really cared for, he asked me at what time would he be expected.

'Seven thirty,' I replied.

'Oh, dear boy,' he said. 'I shall be tucked up in my bed with my hot milk.'

Through my mind went the thought that perhaps I had left it all a bit too late.

'Nevertheless I would very much like to meet you,' he continued to say. You must come down to the Battle of Britain Commemorative Service held on 15th September.'

I was delighted to accept his invitation, what a nice gesture to me a total stranger. This filled me with renewed confidence, perhaps I was not just a sentimental old fool after all.

Wing Commander Ronald Kellett DSO DFC
*Hurricanes and Spitfires 249-303
(Polish) Squadrons, Battle of Britain*

This time as I tapped out his telephone number I felt much more at ease, but still very unsure as to the best way as a total stranger to reassure and at the same time interest him in attending my party. Planned as a special thank you occasion for him, from me who he had never met.

Don't think about it, I thought or your confidence will be lost, just open your mouth and hope for something intelligent to fall out. It felt like trying to sell double glazing over the telephone. So here goes.

The call was answered by a refined female voice, 'No, Mr Kellett is out at the moment, Mrs Kellett speaking.'

I started straight into my now slightly rehearsed explanation for my call. Mrs Kellett listened with apparent interest as I stumbled along, feeling that my description of my party sounded so boring I was not too sure then that even I wanted to attend by now.

Mrs Kellett interrupted my flow with the crushing remark, 'Do be brief, dear boy, my supper is getting cold.'

It felt like an arrow through the heart, steel yourself I thought. I need not have been so concerned, Mrs Kellett despite her crossness at my interruption of her supper, I found later to my delight to be the most kind and gentle of ladies.

My strong point in life has always been tenacity, so stick with it I thought, win through, it's for me to be tolerant, I'm the stranger after all.

The next day found me talking to Ronald Kellett. Yes, he would be delighted to attend the party.

All my setbacks were forgotten by these few words. One

Ronald Kellett, Freddie Parsons, Jimmy Hughes
… very proud of our hero in 1993

Battle of Britain weather vane. Left to right: Frank Cook, President of the Tunbridge Wells R.A.F. Association who flew in Liberators, myself, Group Captain Darley, Colin Taylor, who flew Lancasters; three brave men who were the backbone of the fighter and bomber command problem at eighty four years of age, Ronald no longer drove his car. He was pleased to hear that I would arrange for a car to chauffeur him to my special occasion. Great, my plans were coming together just fine at last.

Wing Commander Michael Ingle-Finch DSO DFC
56 Squadron, Hurricane, Battle of Britain

Once again as I dialled the telephone number a sense of anxiety came over me this must have been one of the most difficult situations to find oneself in, telephoning strangers. I need not have feared at all, a delightful soft cultured voice greeted me.

Mrs Pamela Ingle-Finch had answered the telephone. I was amazed at how quickly she put me at ease. Within minutes she understood my reasons, accepted gracefully my admiration for all her husband had done in 1940.

Michael Ingle-Finch came to the telephone, a quiet-spoken warm voice greeted me. He would very much like to attend the party but unfortunately the date coincided with a pre-planned fishing trip.

Trying to conceal my disappointment I said I hoped we may meet some time at a later date. The very next day once again I listened to Pam Ingle-Finch's warm voice on the telephone, she had rung to ask Beryl and myself to lunch at their home in a beautiful part of Kent. I was delighted to accept, this was much more than I expected. Everything was going so well it was becoming very rewarding for me.

Flight Lieutenant Jimmy Corbin DFC
66 Squadron, Spitfires, Battle of Britain

The telephone rang for some time before a clear and precise voice answered.

'Can I speak to Mr Corbin,' I requested.

'Corbin speaking,' came the reply.

Once again into my now more perfected explanation, I now realised how much my confidence depended on their acceptance. I need not have feared.

'Sounds like a great idea, old boy, love to come, can't I'm afraid, have all my family here from abroad at the moment,' said Jimmy.

I tried to hide my disappointment at this news.

'Much more deserving chaps around than me, old boy,' he continued, an amazingly modest remark for a fighter pilot who in 1940 and for years after had to face the possibility of death every time he climbed into the cockpit of his Spitfire, had to control the gut-churning fear that any normal human beings possess. Jimmy and his Spitfire were very much part of that well oiled finely tuned fighting machine called fighter command and to my mind there was no one more deserving that Flt Lt Jimmy Corbin. As I replaced the telephone receiver I was determined to find a reason to meet Jimmy Corbin sometime soon.

The summer of 1993 had become very important to me, organising the Battle of Britain party, contacting my heroes and also adding one final personal tribute to our few, the construction of a weather vane in honour and depicting in its theme the great battle in the skies over Kent in the hot summer of 1940.

As I set to work designing and putting to paper the ideas in my head, my mind as always went back to that lone Spitfire flying low over the Kent hopfields. That hero, who after doing battle against a ruthless enemy, dived his fighter low over us, wanting to share his excitement with us, the population he was defending—yes, I thought, he shall be the main character to dominate the weather vane. His lone Spitfire driving from our land the Nazi aircraft with their ugly black crosses intent on bringing Britain to her knees.

Freddie, Jimmy Corbin and Jimmy Hughes at the Manston Battle of Britain Museum. In the background Jimmy's Spitfire

Michael Ingle-Finch, my hero and my friend

His Spitfire shall fly forever over the oast houses and churches of the Garden of England, my tribute to this 'One Boy's Hero.'

Throughout the summer of 1993 as the weather vane began to take shape, I was very much aware as I spent hours using steel, heated until white hot, hammered until the shapes became pleasing, lead made molten and them poured into moulds, that the weather vane contained all the vital elements of war, steel, flames, lead, in itself. The weather vane, at last completed, was hoisted into its honoured position high on the pinnacle of Red Cow Farm, Hartley in Kent.

It was with great pleasure that I watched the first flight of my Spitfire as the breeze spun into the wind, our country's most famous fighter, now in its never-ending pursuit of the Messerschmit 109 Hitler's No 1 fighter. As they danced and dived once more over England, this time there would be no escape for the enemy, the Spitfire would be on his tail for eternity.

Below the two fighter planes, a silhouette of the Kent countryside sits like a crown, at the base of the complete weather vane, reads the inscription in moulded lead letters, 'One Boy's Heroes, Our Few'. It was as if I was that seven year old boy again as I looked up at the Spitfire I felt that I had at last said thank you. As interested passers by look up, study and try to analyse the weather vane, they cannot fail to see the inscription and date of 1940. If one person only thinks deeply, their mind drawn as to how much we owe them, that will be reward enough to me.

Party day September 11th 1993 started with massive activity. It was important to me to try to transport my party goers back to the atmosphere of 1940. Suitable music and sound effects were taped, sirens heralding an air raid followed by gunfire and bombs falling were to fill the house. I could almost feel the blast taped windows rattle with the very authentic sound effects. Vera Lynn's clear and wonderful voice would follow through the gunfire, to once again calm us and raise our spirits, no longer the need to sharpen the gramophone needles, now every sound comes from the hi-fi equipment.

On approach to the house large black signs with bold white letters indicating the direction of air raid shelters were posted, others drawing attention to unexploded bombs hung from roped off 'No go' areas. All helped to recreate a wartime feeling, as the party goers filed past sand-bagged blast protection stacked high around the entrance to the house.

Inside the house wartime posters decorated the walls, all with very patriotic slogans, alongside these were large pictures of our fighter command and bomber command aircraft, the scene was set much to the efforts of my family.

The house was full with happy people entering into the spirit of my 1940 period by 8pm, on a pleasant September evening. Some wearing costumes in keeping with the wartime theme which added to the atmosphere considerably.

'He's here,' said Jimmy Hughes. 'I found him wandering around the garden.'

Wing Commander Ronald Kellett had arrived. To my dismay I was unaware and not at the gate to welcome him, how outrageous of me. I immediately thanked him for coming, welcomed him into the warm atmosphere of the oak beamed interior of Red Cow Farm.

After we had exchanged the normal polite greetings, was I now to meet my Spitfire pilot? As his steel blue grey eyes fixed on me I immediately knew he was a man of strong character, there was definitely a Churchillian air to his personality.

Speaking to me as though he was addressing a Squadron debriefing, Ronald hammered home his feelings as to the limitations of aircraft used in the Battle of Britain. his words having all the velocity of the eight machine guns his Hurricane would have used in that great battle, his eighty four years in no way mellowing his personality.

Somewhat taken aback, I searched for less provoking subjects, finding myself feeling quite hesitant and searching hard hoping that I would stumble onto the warm side of Ronald Kellett's personality. I must have said the right thing at last as suddenly his face lit up into a charming smile. What a relief that smile was to me, it was almost a chuckle, as his glass of gin and tonic was raised many times to his lips.

I tried to ask questions in a way that would not make Ronald feel I was only interested in the events of 1940. 'I am sorry to hear your wife is unwell,' I said, knowing she, poor lady, could not attend the party because of having broken her hip early in summer.

'Too bloody slow,' his eyes once more flashing with anger. 'The Hun was faster, we were too slow, was a devil of a job to catch them.'

I was by now totally convinced that Ronald Kellett epitomized in one man all of the determination, boldness and sheer fighting spirit that I would expect from these brave men of the fighter command.

We would attack them from below, break up their formations, then deal with their fighters as the opportunity occurred ... asking him about the first time his thumb pressed the firing button on his eight machine guns in battle. Before he had time to answer I offered to fill his glass once more. Ronald appeared to be enjoying the party, we two strangers both of us coming from backgrounds so different, he very well educated, an officer in the RAF, a highly decorated pilot. Whereas I, a schoolboy from a working class family living in the bombed and blasted London he was defending. Now here we were together, sharing that experience, boy or man, it was our war.

As Ronald lowered his glass to the table he smiled that chuckle-like grin. 'This 109 fighter came into my sights, instead of diving away from me as he should have, the darn fool pulled up, giving me a perfect shot.'

Ronald's first kill, I shall never know how many other Nazi invaders never returned home because of Ronald's brave engagements.

'Never recorded my claims, didn't feel the need to,' he remarked.

There was something in Ronald Kellett's character that I immediately recognised as true British Bulldog spirit. What would we have done without that boldness in 1940. As we were getting on so well Ronald and I helped no doubt by our now once again empty glasses, I felt this was the right moment to mention my Spitfire, could it have been Ronald flying low that day.

Once again I had triggered a sensitive spot on Ronald's memory. His face thundered over, eyes flashed at me, in their now quite familiar way. 'I would have court-marshalled him, damned fool,' said Ronald. 'Stupid thing to do, a victory roll after battle, his lines could have been shot through'.

Of course Ronald was quite right and I was aware that this behaviour was frowned upon by pilots' commanding officers for the very reasons he stated.

'You were never tempted to victory roll your fighter, Ronald,' I asked. 'Even if there were cartloads of pretty young land army girls waving at you from the fields below.'

'Never,' he bellowed. I would never argue with that Churchillian glare, I wouldn't dare. I was totally convinced by now that Ronald could easily have fought the entire German Luftwaffer on his own. Such was this man's strength of character, perhaps if the Nazi bombers had met Ronald as I had, speaking over their aircraft intercom, they would have yelled instead of 'Auchtung Spitfire', 'Auchtung Ronald Kellett'.

I am still not too sure whether Ronald would have Victory rolled his aircraft on that hot summer's day in 1940, I noticed a definite twinkle in his eye when in the company of ladies, perhaps the temptation to break the rules might have occurred to him just once.

Around us both, the party was in full swing. It was time for my presentation and thank you speech. As the noise of the party fell to a hush, my wife Beryl entered the room holding a large white iced cake, its blue candles shaped in a large 'V' for victory twinkling in the darkened room, around the candles read the inscription 'One Boy's Heroes, Our Few'.

As I introduced my boyhood friends, told stories of our life in 1940, my arm was around the shoulder of my hero Ronald Kellett. As the champagne bottles popped and to cheers of 'he's a jolly good fellow', I said to Ronald and it was from my heart, 'thank you for all you did in 1940.'

His reply, 'Sorry we didn't do better.' He smiled that warm smile followed by a subdued chuckle.

I was reduced to silence by such a modest remark, but then that is what one would expect from his generation.

As Ronald left my home that night, laden down with a bouquet of flowers for Mrs Kellett, a framed photo of my weather vane suitably inscribed, I felt a deep satisfaction. It really had been worthwhile to try and fulfil a dream, before time the greatest enemy of all closes the book.

As my guests grew tired of dancing to the Andrew Sisters, singing along with Vera Lynn, an air raid siren sounded for the last time. Sounds of guns firing, aircraft roaring overhead, bombs dropping on a make-believe London, slowly died from the hi-fi speakers. All had now become quiet. We recreated a moment in time, and as the last guest left, I realised it had been a great success.

The party now over, Sunday found me at a Tunbridge Wells Church attending the Battle of Britain Memorial Service, having been invited to meet Group Capt. Darley DSO DFC Battle of Britain there. Throughout the service I had been searching the congregation in forlorn hope of recognising him. This was quite impossible as there was a sea of medals glinting in the shafts of bright light entering the church windows that day.

Which one was my hero I thought, deciding to seek the help of the vicar. 'Have you seen Group Capt Darley?'

The vicar asked around, 'Yes, he arrived late and sat quietly at the back,' said a distinguished grey-haired man who guided me into the outer chambers of the church. There I came face to face with Group Capt Darley, he greeted me warmly with an air of total gentleness, as I shook hands with him my thoughts were, such a gentle man having to fight in the bloody arena of September 1940.

He showed great interest in my commemorative weather vane accepting the framed copy with a 'thank you, how kind'.

We were now surrounded by interested members of the RAF Association.

'Thank you for all you did in 1940,' I said. 'We are very proud of you.'

To my delight the grey-haired distinguished gentleman muttered, 'how nice, what a nice gesture'.

Before Group Capt Darley was whisked away to meet dignitaries at this reception, he looked me straight in the eye, drawing closer to me he whispered, 'why did you use the Messerschmitt 109 in your weather vane?'.

I looked back at him quizzically.

'It was the bombers that we were after you know, it was always the bombers.'

As he was gently led away from me by the RAF chaplain saying, 'you must come and meet the mayor', we exchanged smiles. I was but one of his many admirers that day but to me this brave man was symbolic of all that embraced the spirit of 1940.

It was with great expectations that Beryl and I arrived at the door of Wing Commander Michael Ingle-Finch, a pretty country cottage in a most beautiful part of Kent. We had been invited to lunch by Michael and Pam, a more than kind gesture to offer to total strangers, that had made contact with them earlier with odd stories of heroes and weather vanes. Warmly greeted, we were shown into a very comfortable and cosy room, the sun on this beautiful day shining brightly through their bay windows.

I was immediately impressed by Michael a tall handsome man who one felt at ease with instantly. Pam, a tall slender, most beautiful woman, showing all the gentleness that she had conveyed during our telephone conversation.

'Tell me about the party and the weather vane,' said Pam enthusiastically.

We sat back in their comfortable chairs, pre-lunch drink in hand, Pam having the priceless gift to make one feel that every utterance, no matter how trivial, is about to be followed with a pearl of wisdom. She immediately understood my sentiments towards Battle of Britain pilots and for the very first time I felt I had found a real soulmate.

Michael listened, nodded, mumbled an embarrassed how nice from time to time, as I explained just how vivid the memories of a small boys were. When the black shape of Nazi bombers flew low over South East London, it was his Hurricane that wove the vapour trails in determined and brave defiance in the blue sky above my London. I felt proud to be in the company of such a man as Michael Ingle-Finch. A modest but self assured sensitive character, this great country of ours produced men such as Michael at a time when we needed them most. When Winston Churchill said in reply to Hitler's threats, what kind of people do they think we are, he knew that people like Michael would show Nazi Germany just exactly what kind of people we were. Michael's 56 Squadron flew from North Weald Airfield and took part in some terrific battles being involved in as many as seven sorties a day, seven times to face possible death.

Michael started his flying career before the war in 1938, this man was perfecting his flying skills that were to hold him in such good stead, when fate found him fighting for his life in the cockpit of his Hurricane, weaving that web of vapour trails that we saw so often in the skies over Kent.

'What was it like up there, fighting for your country Michael,' I asked, realising as I said it that it could have been phrased much better.

'Terrifying,' he said. In a word he had made me feel even more admiration for men in that despite their natural human fears, knew Britain needed them so much in our most desperate hour.

As Michael and I chatted on about the war years my mind drifted away to that rotating fighter. Could it have been Michael that day? He certainly fitted my imaginary figure of a daring fighter pilot, handsome, unflappable, determined, yes, I think he would probably have done something like that in a moment of exhilaration and success.

As we said farewell to Michael and Pam that day, I was left with the strong feeling that people of their generation had that something special, they had a sense of honour and dedication. That seems so hard to find now, yet it is the same blood that flows in the present generation. I like to feel that if Britain ever needed them once again our young people would show an aggressor just what kind of people we are.

Flt Lt Jimmy Corbin's invitation to visit him was somewhat contrived by me with a telephone call. 'Could I call in to see you, Mr Corbin?' I enquired. 'I would very much like to present you with a framed photo of my Battle of Britain commemorative weather vane.'

'Of course, old boy,' he said, 'anytime.'

A few days later found Beryl and I arriving in their driveway, slightly unsure as to if we were at the right address. A very attractive lady, trimming the roses at the time, greeted us.

'Do come in,' said Jeanne, Jimmy's wife. 'He is expecting you.'

Jeanne moved ahead of us with all the grace and good looks of a Vogue magazine model. Amazing, I thought, these fighter pilots do have the charisma to attract beautiful women.

Jimmy Corbin rose to great us, a tall man with a broad mischievous grin shook my hand warmly. Jimmy had flown Spitfires with 610 and 66 Squadrons in the Battle of Britain, was himself again a flyer with the RAAF before the war in 1939. Sitting in his lounge sipping tea, was very enjoyable for me and I intended to savour every moment of his company. Conversation flowed very easily, we were all instantly at ease allowing a very jolly atmosphere to prevail.

Jimmy started his career with Fighter Command as a sergeant pilot, was later commissioned and continued to fly as Flt Left, later as Squadron Leader. As I studied Jimmy's personality I found a strong determined character with plenty of drive, very down-to-earth in his thinking. Here was a man that had no intention of backing down against the Hun in that hot summer of 1940, here was a man highly skilled in air gunnery and later to become an instructor to impart his battle skills to other pilots.

'Being alert helped you stay alive you know,' he said.

Of course he was quite right, high-scoring fighter pilots only became so if they stayed alive long enough to accumulate such a high score.

'When one saw those yellow noses of the Messerschmitt 109 high above, you certainly had to watch out,' he continued. 'Especially if your position was at the rear of your Squadron's attack.'

'Was it difficult to keep your nerve, when bombers returned your fire?' I asked.

Jimmy gave me that broad grin of his as he replied, 'Didn't worry me too much, old boy, they only had one machine gun and I had eight.'

I was very much aware that to question these brave men on their exploits could be tedious for them, answering the same type of questions for over fifty years now. To people like me, I was very anxious not to be as perhaps the others had been before me. As the age gap between us had narrowed over the years, from the time I was a boy and he a young man, we now talked of the war as people—he just somewhat older than me—it was our war and in that war this man was my hero. Without the Jimmy Corbins, Hitler would have turned London into ashes, bombed and battered by day and night. We as Londoners had learned how to take it, but without our fighter command, the Luftwaffer would have been able to bomb with impunity, living among all that bombing each day seeing more whole streets disappear into just rubble, it must not be difficult for you to understand our love and admiration for our boys in the sky.

As our afternoon visit drew to an end my thoughts as always returned to that Spitfire and the way we cheered him from the sun scorched fields in that late summer of 1940. Yes, I thought you most definitely would have victory rolled your Spitfire, Jimmy.

Jimmy Corbin had all the qualities needed in a fighter pilot, calculating confidence and courage, excellent flying skills and one other ingredient that to my mind would have made him tempted to break the rules ... The temptation to gain the admiration of those pretty girls in the field below would have overcome any fear of reprisal that may have come from his superior officers.

He gave me this final clue when in conversation he said, 'Rank never worried me old boy'. Combine this remark with the crushing hug he gave Beryl as we left that day, 'He always liked little blondes,' said Jeanne laughing ... yes, there was a loveable element of rascal in Jimmy that I am sure would have completed the ingredient.

As we said our goodbyes that afternoon I left with a special feeling for Jimmy Corbin.

'I too went hop picking with my grandmother when I was a boy,' he said in conversation. 'Great fun,' he chuckled.

What an achievement, I thought from a boy picking hops with his grandmother to a university education, then to become a fighter command pilot, must have demanded supreme determination.

So now I had met all my heroes. They, I know, would not wish to accept that description. A hero is a man that goes beyond his duty, remarked Ronald Kellett. 'I just did my duty as my country naturally expected of me.'

I know all my heroes would agree with Ronald, they would not for one minute consider themselves as heroes, but they must forgive me for disagreeing with them, facing the fear of death and destruction day after day, knowing that if you were found lacking, your country would fall under the heel of a tyrant that the world had not seen the like of since the mongol hoards had butchered their way into the history books. These men I call heroes.

As my story now comes closer to its end, I apologise for not perhaps having the writing ability of George Bernard Shaw, the drama of Shakespeare and certainly not Winston Churchill's power of delivery. But then it is important to understand that these words were those of a schoolboy whose thoughts transported him back to those war years of the 1940s.

No matter how old we get, the little boy never quite leaves us, he is still in the memory. The happiness of childhood is magical. Mine was no exception ... without the fears of my parents, my childhood was a paradise of war. Rubbled streets, dark nights, bombers overhead, we quickly learned to accept as everyday events. Nothing worried us boys, life was too exciting. Our playground was amongst bricks and rubble, and we had all the materials easily at hand to transport our minds one day on a pirate ship, the next we would be fighter pilots, sitting in an old tin bath, with chair legs as our machine guns—imagining we were up there in the deep blue sky fighting for England just as our heroes were doing in 1940.

My true story now completed, I hope I have achieved my goal to log these events for future generations of my family and hopefully to entertain the reader along the way. In my quest for my hero I feel I did find him in the end. I think he was a combination of all the qualities of all four pilots.

I like to think of him as he bravely fought that day, as having the aggressive boldness of Ronald Kellett, combined with the dashing good looks and modesty of Michael Ingle-Finch. The gentleness and wisdom of Group Captain Darley, add to these the tenacity, determination and cheeky smile of Jimmy Corbin.

We could not have been in safer hands.